THE YANKS ARE COMING

THE YANKS ARE COMING

The United States in the First World War

Albert Marrin

BEAUTIFUL FEET BOOKS, INC.
SAN LUIS OBISPO, CALIFORNIA

ISBN 1-893103-11-0
Library of Congress Contol Number: 2002105485

Photograph credits:
All photographs are courtesy of The National Archives except as noted below.
Bundesarchive, Koblenz, 5; Defense Department: page 124
Imperial War Museum, London: pages 90, 103 and 137
Library of Congress: page 32
Author's collection: pages 3, 18, 19, 40, 95, 99, 147, 173 and 176

Cover illustration by Viqui Maggio
Copyright © Viqui Maggio

Printed in the United States of America

Published by Beautiful Feet Books, Inc.
1306 Mill Street
San Luis Obispo, CA 93401

www.bfbooks.com
800.889.1978

This book is dedicated, affectionately,
to the Doughboys.

"It is a fearful thing to lead this great
peaceful people into war, into the most terrible
and disastrous of all wars, civilization itself
seeming to be in the balance."

WOODROW WILSON,
War Message, April 2, 1917

Contents

vii

Contents

THE YANKS
ARE COMING

Prelude:
The Passing
of a Sea Queen

✯ Friday, May 7, 1915. The Atlantic Ocean ten miles south of the Old Head of Kinsale, Ireland. A dazzling afternoon with a cloudless sky and the sea smooth as glass. Visibility unlimited.

The proud ocean liner plows ahead, bound for her home port of Liverpool, England. Her four red smokestacks, each large enough for a coach and horses to drive through, belch clouds of white smoke. Her name, painted in golden letters a foot high on her black hull, glints in the sunlight: LUSITANIA.

She's a beauty, the largest and fastest liner of her time. If stood upright, her 785 feet would tower thirty-four feet above the United States Capitol. At over thirty thousand tons, she's heavier than any battleship of the day. Yet, despite her size, she can race along at twenty-five knots (thirty-one miles) an hour, leaving behind any but the swiftest warships.

It has been an uneventful voyage since the *Lusitania* sailed from New York six days ago. Aboard the ship are 1,924 people, crew and passengers, including 197 Americans. The passengers spend their time as they would in any first-class

3

hotel ashore. They amuse themselves on deck with shuffle-board contests, potato sack races, and long walks in the salt air. Below decks they play cards, dance to the fox-trot band in the lounge, or just sit around the gorgeously decorated parlors and smoking rooms. Occasionally there is a brief lifeboat drill, which few take seriously. The voyage is so normal, so ordinary, that a passenger pipes up, "It's been such a dull, dreary, stupid trip! I can't help hoping that we get some sort of thrill going up the channel."

Just over the horizon, several miles away, a submarine lies on the surface. The U-20—*Unterseeboot* or undersea boat-20—bobs gently, her deck awash in case she has to make a quick getaway. Walther Schwieger stands in the conning tower, scanning the empty sea through binoculars. Blond and blue-eyed, the thirty-two-year-old Schwieger is one of the most beloved captains in the German submarine service. He runs a happy boat, for nothing is too good for his crew. Although food is scarce, he makes sure, one way or another, that they eat well. The latest phonograph records help pass the time in their stainless steel prison. He even allows pet dogs aboard, and one is nursing her pups in a corner of the radio shack.

U-20 sailed on April 30, a day before the *Lusitania*. It had been a disappointing patrol. Pickings were skimpy. Apart from two small steamers and a wooden sailing ship, there hadn't been anything worth sinking. Schwieger was about to call it quits and plot a course for home when four red smokestacks appeared over the horizon.

The blare of the diving alarm startles the crew into action. Hatches slam shut with a metallic clang. Sea valves snap open, flooding ballast tanks. Within a minute fading ripples are all that mark the U-boat's position. Only the tip of the periscope peers above the surface, an oversized glass eye, cold, staring, menacing.

The *Lusitania* comes on boldly, blind to the peril lurking a half-mile away. Schwieger, his eye glued to the periscope, follows her every movement. Softly, as if talking to himself, he gives bearings to the wheelman, who controls the rudder and hydroplanes, the submarine's "fins."

In the torpedo room below, the air is heavy with moisture and the odor of sweat, unwashed feet, and machine oil. The torpedoes, twenty-one feet long and cigar-shaped, rest in racks along the wall. Their handlers know them by nicknames like Shining Emma, Bertha, and Yellow Mary. But there is nothing cute or funny about these silvery packages.

As the liner comes to the center of the periscope's cross-hairs, Schwieger says just one word: *"Feur!"*—fire. The sub-

Walter Schwieger, skipper of the U-20, which torpedoed the Lusitania, *bringing about the worst civilian sea disaster of the First World War.*

marine jolts upward for a moment, suddenly lightened by a ton of dead weight. It is exactly 2:09 P.M.

Aboard the *Lusitania*, a lookout atop his high perch sees an arrow of bubbling white water. Grabbing a megaphone, he shouts toward the captain's bridge, "Torpedo coming on the starboard side!" After that he can do nothing but watch the torpedo punch a hole in the vessel's right side and disappear.

For a split second nothing happens. Then the delayed-action fuse fires the main charge in the warhead. The muffled rumble of the torpedo is followed by a second, thunderous, roar. The decks seem to rise, then settle. People are lifted off their feet and flung about like rag dolls. A geyser of steam, water, coal, wood, and metal fragments gushes a hundred feet above the radio mast then splatters to the promenade deck.

The torpedo entered the boiler room area between the first and second smokestacks, smashing at least one boiler filled with steam under high pressure. The exploding boiler had the force of a bomb the size of a railway car going off in a sealed tunnel. Instantly the *Lusitania*'s bow blew apart. Power lines snapped. Steering control failed. Lights went out, plunging the belowdeck spaces into blackness. Passengers were trapped in elevators between decks.

Regaining their feet, people noticed that the floor was at a strange angle. As the *Lusitania*'s bow slipped under, she listed to starboard; that is, tilted forward and to the right. In order to stand erect, you had to walk on part of the walls. It was the start of one of history's greatest sea disasters.

People stampeded to get into the lifeboats, although few succeeded. The *Lusitania* developed a sharp list so quickly that the lifeboats on the port (left) side swung inward,

"All the News That's
Fit to Print."

The New York Times.

EXTRA
8:30 A.M.

VOL. LXIV NO. 20,916   NEW YORK, SATURDAY, MAY 8, 1915—TWENTY-FOUR PAGES.   ONE CENT

LUSITANIA SUNK BY A SUBMARINE, PROBABLY 1,260 DEAD; TWICE TORPEDOED OFF IRISH COAST; SINKS IN 15 MINUTES; CAPT. TURNER SAVED, FROHMAN AND VANDERBILT MISSING; WASHINGTON BELIEVES THAT A GRAVE CRISIS IS AT HAND

This drawing on the front page of The New York Times *gives an accurate picture of the ocean liner listing to starboard as she sinks by the bow.*

smashing themselves against the hull. The starboard lifeboats swung out and downward, so that only six could be launched properly. Unable to use the lifeboats, hundreds of people fell or jumped screaming into the sea.

The sounds of the dying ship were terrifying. Groans and moans came from heavy timbers and steel plates struggling to become separated. There was the crashing of boilers and cargo tearing loose and tumbling toward the bow; it sounded like a huge hardware store turned upside down and shaken. And always there was the swish and gurgle of water swirling through the flooding passageways.

People floundering in the water looked up and saw an unforgettable sight. The liner, tilting sharply downward, stood almost straight up, balancing for a moment on her bow, which had struck the ocean floor. Her stern hovered high above their heads, its four propellers nearly motionless, the sixty-ton rudder flopping aimlessly. As she settled, the number 3 boiler exploded, carrying away its smokestack in a cloud of steam. When the steam cleared, the *Lusitania* was gone.

In her place the sea was covered with splintered lifeboats, luggage, tables, chairs, bottles, barrels, bales, bundles, bits of clothing, and bodies. It was 2:27 P.M., eighteen minutes after Schwieger fired his torpedo. Rescuers later recovered 1,198 bodies, including the remains of 128 Americans. This was a "victory" Germany would long regret.

ONE

War Comes to America

Even though their country was at peace, those Americans who went down with the *Lusitania* weren't the first to die in this way, nor would they be the last. The United States was an innocent bystander in a struggle that was drawing her in as surely as whirpools draw fallen leaves.

War had been raging since July 1914. People called this struggle by various names: Great War, World War, First World War. Not that they believed, then, that there would be a Second World War. They used the term First World War because this was the first time that a war had been fought on a worldwide scale. War is as old as civilization. Yet no war had ever involved nations from every continent. Never before had battles been fought in the air as well as on the land, on the seas as well as beneath them.

The causes of the First World War go back at least to 1870, when Germany defeated France in an earlier conflict. Although a treaty ended this war, it failed to make peace between these long-time enemies. Each nation hated and

9

feared the other. France hated Germany for taking away the
territories of Alsace and Lorraine, while Germany feared
that one day France would attack her in revenge.

Germany, however, was by far the more powerful country. The basis of her power was heavy industry and a military
machine directed by the kaiser, or emperor. Under the kaiser,
the factory owners and generals ruled the nation with an
iron hand.

Even so, imperial Germany was nothing like the Nazi
dictatorship later built by Adolf Hitler. There was no
Gestapo (secret police) to crush opposition or concentration
camps where people were murdered for their political or
religious beliefs. Imperial Germany had a parliament that,
like our Congress, made the laws. There were free elections,
political parties, and labor unions. But despite these, no really
important decisions could be made without the consent of
the kaiser and his advisers. Kaiser Wilhelm II had ruled
Germany since 1888. A fierce-looking man with a walrus
mustache, he liked to be called "All-Highest" and "Supreme
War Lord." He was forever boasting about his army and
calling upon his troops to act like Huns, an ancient tribe
noted for its savagery.

Hatred and fear drove both France and Germany into finding ways to strengthen themselves. Alliances were formed.
A group of nations, most notably Russia and Italy, known
as the Allies clustered around France. Great Britain, although
not bound by a treaty, had an *"Entente Cordiale,"* or "polite
understanding," to aid France if necessary. Germany's
friends, called the Central Powers, because they were located
in Central Europe, were Austria-Hungary and Bulgaria,
joined later by Turkey. Each country had its own reason
for taking sides: to have friends in case of war, to protect its

trade, to help gain colonies overseas. The British Empire—
Canada, Australia, New Zealand, South Africa, India—
Japan, and a host of Latin American countries later joined
the Allies.

Then, as now, statesmen believed that weapons could help
nations get what they wanted and keep what they had. An
arms race began in which each nation's taxpayers were asked
to spend billions to keep up with would-be enemies. It was
a race not in atomic weapons, but to build up million-man
armies, reserves of artillery, and mighty battle fleets.

The result of the buildup was the opposite of what was
intended. More armaments made people feel less secure. And
the only way to get over that feeling for a while was to
increase the next year's weapons budget. Europe became a
fireworks warehouse guarded by careless watchmen.

*His Imperial Majesty,
Kaiser Wilhelm II, Emperor
of Germany. His haughty
manner and fierce mustache
gave Americans a fright.*

Someone lit the match on June 28, 1914. On that day a terrorist assassinated the Austrian Archduke Francis Ferdinand and his wife during a visit to Sarajevo in Bosnia, a tiny country now part of Yugoslavia. The Austrians blamed neighboring Serbia, now also part of Yugoslavia, for the murder of the heir to the Austrian throne. Such a cowardly act, they felt, had to be punished by a full-scale invasion. National honor demanded nothing less than war.

Austria's war with Serbia set the alliances in motion. Russia, eager to aid its "little brother," Serbia, moved its army to the Austrian border, threatening a counterinvasion. Kaiser Wilhelm II warned the Russian emperor, Czar Nicholas II, to back off—or else. France, meanwhile, prepared to help its Russian friend.

With war drawing near, the kaiser decided to land the first blow. On August 3, 1914, he sent his army crashing through Belgium. His generals planned to use Belgium, which belonged to no alliance, as a shortcut to Paris, bypassing the French armies massed along the border. By occupying the French capital quickly, he hoped to force a surrender, allowing most of the German army to rush east to fight the Russians. The war was expected to end by Christmas in victory for the Central Powers.

It didn't. The German timetable, so carefully worked out on paper, was upset by Great Britain. No sooner had war begun, than the British sent an army to help the French and Belgians. The British felt that they could never be safe with the victorious Germans just across the English Channel, a stone's throw from their seaports. By invading Belgium, the kaiser had also broken a treaty in which the major powers promised to respect Belgian neutrality in any war. The treaty, said the Germans, was merely a "scrap of paper" to be ignored when convenient. If so, Britain could never expect Germany to keep its word about anything.

Things went badly for the Allies from the beginning, although not badly enough to give the enemy a quick victory. Within weeks the Germans overran most of Belgium and were driving toward Paris. Only desperate fighting, with hundreds of thousands of casualties, killed and wounded, was able to halt them along the Marne River, almost within sight of the capital. Slowly the French pushed back the invaders, saving Paris, although the northern and eastern part of the country remained in German hands.

Then everything seemed to stand still. The war became a stalemate with neither side able to strike the knockout blow. Christmas 1914 found the armies dug into trench lines stretching unbroken for five hundred miles from the Swiss border to the North Sea. Millions of men lived and died in these hellholes of mud and blood during the next four years. Alfred Joubaire, a French officer, wrote in his diary shortly before he was killed: "Humanity is mad! It must be mad to do what it is doing. What a massacre! What scenes of horror and bloodshed! Hell cannot be so terrible. Men are mad!"

Americans watched the madness from a distance, thankful to be on the far shore of the Atlantic. Neutrality was the official policy of the nation. Of course we had treaties with foreign governments, but none bound us to go to war. Ever since George Washington warned against "entangling alliances," no president had made an alliance with a foreign country. Americans wanted nothing better than to stay out of other peoples' wars, and for others to keep out of our troubles.

When the First World War began, Woodrow Wilson,

twenty-eighth President of the United States, pledged neutrality. He was so careful about not taking sides that, rumor
said, sailors were forbidden to whistle "It's a Long Way to
Tipperary," a popular British marching song. Privately, however, Wilson's heart was with the Allies. He hated German
boasting and bluster, their trust in force as the easy answer
to problems. He feared that if the Allies lost, America would
have to stop being a democracy and use all her energies for
defense.

The American people were more outspoken than their
president. In countless speeches and newspaper articles, they
came out in favor of the Allies, especially Great Britain. To
this day ties between the United States and the Mother
Country are very strong. English is our national language.
Our laws, courts, and system of representative government
are based on English models. People believed that the Allies
were fighting for the same things Americans cherished. The
kaiser frightened them. In the words of an anonymous poet:

> *Kaiser, Kaiser shining bright*
> *You have given us a fright*
> *With your belts and straps and sashes,*
> *And your skyward-turned mustaches!*
> *Kaiser, Kaiser Man of War*
> *What a fearful man you are!*

If the kaiser could get away with invading a small, peaceful
country like Belgium, the world would become a jungle. And
in the jungle violence is the only law.

War did not mean that Americans had to cut themselves
off from the rest of the world. As neutrals, and as a leading
industrial power, they wanted to trade with all nations alike.
Industrialists were willing to sell anything to anyone who'd

pay their prices. American ships were forbidden to carry war matériel, for that would have meant taking sides. Yet it was perfectly legal to sell weapons and munitions so long as the warring nations took them away in their own ships.

Then, Great Britain, the world's leading naval power, clamped a blockade around Germany. Swift destroyers swept German merchantmen from the seas. The Grand Fleet, scores of big-gunned battleships and cruisers, bottled up German fighting ships in their ports. The one time the German navy came out to do battle, at Jutland in 1916, it was beaten back with heavy losses. The next time it put to sea was to surrender to the victorious Allies at the end of the war.

The British tightened their blockade at every opportunity. The War Office in London declared a long list of goods contraband, illegal even for neutral ships to bring to Germany. In addition to guns and ammunition, the list included anything that might help the enemy war effort: machinery, chemicals, petroleum products, cloth. Even food was on the list, for enemy workers and warriors must eat.

Neutral vessels were stopped on the high seas and searched from stem to stern. If contraband was found, the vessel was taken to a British port and its cargo sold for Allied use. Shippers were paid for their goods, although at much lower prices than the Germans offered. Mailbags were also seized and letters read by intelligence officers looking for enemy spy messages and any information useful to the Allied military.

American ships were treated as any other neutral's by the blockaders. People became angry, not so much over lost profits, but at the insult to the flag. Protests flew across the Atlantic, landing with the force of paper bullets. The British listened politely, said they were sorry for the inconvenience to their American friends, and tightened the blockade. The Allies were fighting for their lives and would do whatever they thought necessary, no matter what others might say. Besides, they reminded our ambassador, the British blockade hurt no Americans, but the Germans were killing them.

They were right. Germany's answer to the blockade was to declare a "war zone" around the British Isles. Unable to match the Grand Fleet gun for gun, they rushed construction of a fleet of submarines; at its height the fleet had 128 vessels. These tiny undersea craft easily slipped between, or *under*, the blockaders and steered for the shipping lanes.

Any Allied vessel found in the forbidden area was fair game, liable to be sunk without warning. Since submarines had neither the space to hold survivors nor carried enough food to feed them, there could be no rescues. Survivors were on their own, to sink or swim. It became normal to see tankers blazing far out to sea at night, casting an orange glow on the low-hanging clouds. The waters around the British Isles became a junkyard of floating wreckage. So as not to give the U-boats targets, vessels were ordered to plow through the wreckage at high speed, stopping for nothing.

In the eyes of U-boat captains, a merchantman or a passenger liner was the same as a warship. If it was right for the British "starvation blockade" to kill German people slowly, then, they reasoned, it was right for them to kill their enemies quickly by drowning. Nor was it always possible to spare neutrals. If neutrals sailed on British ships, they did so at their own risk; the Germans had no intention of allowing Allied vessels free passage because they might have neutrals aboard. If neutral ships entered the war zone and were mistaken for Allied vessels—well, that was their problem. Such mistakes might easily happen, since the British used neutral flags to deceive the undersea raiders. U-boat victories were applauded in Germany, and the top-scoring captains were treated as heroes.

Americans began to suffer from the counterblockade. When their ships were sunk, the Germans apologized for the "error" and offered to pay damages. By twos and threes, American passengers died on torpedoed Allied merchantmen. The *Lusitania,* the greatest disaster of all, only highlighted the tragedy of the First World War.

Before the *Lusitania* sailed, the German government placed ads in American newspapers warning passengers that she was sailing into a war zone and might be torpedoed. Few heeded the warning. They might have acted differently had they known, as was later revealed, that the liner carried a secret cargo: hundreds of tons of rifle bullets and artillery shells.

Everyone thought themselves in the right; that's the tragedy of war. The British were right to gamble with civilians' lives to protect a cargo needed to fight in a just cause. The Germans were right to sink enemy vessels after giving due warning. The American passengers were right to insist that, as neutrals, they should be protected wherever they sailed. The result of all these "rights" was a disaster in which all suffered.

A storm of outrage swept the United States after the *Lusitania* sinking. "Murder!" screamed newspaper headlines. Cartoons showed U-boat captains as smirking killers enjoying their victims' pain. Ghosts of drowned children were shown pointing to the kaiser and asking, "But why did you kill *us?*" Many demanded war to punish this cowardly act.

All eyes turned to the President during the crisis. What would Woodrow Wilson do? Where would he lead? The nation waited, and wondered.

Those who expected him to lead straight into war didn't

NOTICE!

TRAVELLERS intending to embark on the Atlantic voyage are reminded that a state of war exists between Germany and her allies and Great Britain and her allies; that the zone of war includes the waters adjacent to the British Isles; that, in accordance with formal notice given by the Imperial German Government, vessels flying the flag of Great Britain, or of any of her allies, are liable to destruction in those waters and that travellers sailing in the war zone on ships of Great Britain or her allies do so at their own risk.

IMPERIAL GERMAN EMBASSY
WASHINGTON, D. C., APRIL 22, 1915.

Warning. The Germans printed this warning in many newspapers in order to dissuade Americans from sailing on the Lusitania. *Few heeded their advice.*

know their man. Wilson hated war with all his soul. It had always been that way. The first thing he could remember about his life concerned war, the Civil War. At the age of three, he'd stood at the door of the family home in Augusta, Georgia, as passersby yelled, "Mr. Lincoln's elected. There'll be *war!*" Puzzled, he toddled into Father Wilson's study to ask, "What is war?"

He found out soon enough. Georgia became a battleground. General Sherman's Union Army burned and blasted its way across the state on a march to the sea. Lines of retreating Confederate soldiers, whipped and miserable, trudged wearily past the Wilson house.

The boy, now grown to a man of fifty-nine, was haunted by visions of war. Those visions didn't make him cowardly, only cautious. It might be necessary to fight Germany one day. If that day came, the President knew he could lead the nation through the terrible time. But in 1915, he was unwilling to give up on peace so easily. He'd try everything, do anything, to keep peace with honor. The lives of millions of young men required that he do nothing less.

On May 10, three days after the *Lusitania* disaster, President Wilson addressed a gathering of new citizens. It was a startling speech, not once mentioning Germany or the *Lusitania*. Indeed, he spoke with deep feeling of the nation's devotion to peace and how it must be an example to the world. We were neutral. Remaining neutral was so right that there was no need to convince others of its rightness by force. He ended with a memorable phrase: "There is such a thing as a man being too proud to fight."

Opponents gasped. Why, a man, a real man, would be too proud *not* to fight. Theodore Roosevelt sputtered and fumed. "TR," a former president and hero of the Spanish-American War of 1898, never forgave Wilson for this speech. "Flubdubs and mollycoddles," he thundered; Wilson and his fol-

Ex-President Theodore Roosevelt denounced Woodrow Wilson for not asking for a declaration of war after the sinking of the Lusitania.

lowers were bunglers and sissies unfit to lead a proud people.

Wilson closed his ears to demands for war. In the months that followed, he sent several messages to the kaiser's government. Their tone was polite, although filled with hard words and stern warnings. The president made it clear that American ships had a right to go wherever they pleased, their flag acting as a safe-conduct pass; American citizens must be allowed to travel in safety anywhere. If not, we'd "sever diplomatic relations" with the German Empire, a polite term for declaring war.

Germany took the hint. In April 1916, it ordered its U-boats not to sink merchantmen without warning and to do everything possible to rescue crews and passengers. It was a victory for Wilson, much-appreciated by the American people. In November they elected him to a second term as President on the slogan, "He Kept Us Out of War." He had—for the moment.

The Germans put a leash on their submarines because they didn't want to fight the United States. Yet they felt that Wilson had been unfair, forcing them to fight with one hand tied. For once they spared merchantmen, American-made war matériel began to flow unchecked to the Allies. Unable to stop these supplies on the high seas, they decided to cut them off at the source. The United States was about to become the battleground in a secret war.

The German Embassy in Washington, D.C., was turned into a base for spies and saboteurs. Money was no problem. Count von Bernstorff, the ambassador, had over one hundred million dollars in cash to use however he thought best in the United States. He spent freely, knowing that he had only to ask for more millions to be delivered; as ambassador he enjoyed diplomatic immunity, meaning that he was free from

Captain Franz von Papen was one of the master spies working out of the German Embassy in Washington before the United States entered the war.

arrest for any reason and that packages sent to him couldn't be searched by United States customs.

Von Bernstorff personally tried his hand at troublemaking. He sent a message to Berlin asking permission to bribe members of Congress with up to fifty thousand dollars each. Such bribes, he hoped, would influence congressmen to speak against President Wilson's stand. The message, however, fell into the hands of the State Department, which made it public. Von Bernstorff stammered an apology and handed over undercover work to experts.

Three of the ambassador's aides were brilliant agents. Captain Franz von Papen was a soldier who later helped Hitler's rise to power. Captain Carl Boy-Ed, a navy man, knew his way around the United States as if it were his own country. Naval Commander Franz von Rintelen, handsome, intelligent and sly as a fox, was Germany's chief spymaster on this side of the Atlantic.

Together the three organized a network of agents that stretched from coast to coast. Their agents were of different types. Some were professionals trained at spy and sabotage schools in Germany. Others were Americans angry at their country for one reason or another and willing to betray it for a price. Spies specialized in gaining secret information about military plans, American and Allied, and shipments of war matériel. Saboteurs knew how to destroy or damage those shipments before they reached Europe.

These German spies were a failure, never stealing an important American secret. The Secret Service, which usually protects the president and tracks down counterfeiters, kept close tabs on suspected agents. These agents were so busy evading detection that they had little time for spying. MI6, Britain's secret intelligence service, was also helpful. British code breakers had learned to read most German codes and were only too happy to pass useful information to the Secret Service.

Saboteurs were more successful than spies. Loners who kept to themselves and had plenty of money, they were difficult to catch unless they made serious mistakes. Americans gained a healthy respect for German saboteurs, something they'd carry over into the Second World War. The complete story of German sabotage in this country in 1915–1917 has never been told. It probably *cannot* be told, because saboteurs seldom wrote about their activities or filed formal reports. What is known, though, is chilling enough.

Saboteurs used the United States as a laboratory for germ warfare. The head of this project was a German-American doctor of medicine named Anton Degler. When the war began, Degler, who was traveling in Germany, offered his services to the army intelligence corps. After a brief training period, his superiors gave him vials of live glanders and an-thrax bacteria, both highly contagious diseases of horses, sheep, cattle, and sometimes humans.

Degler's target was horses and mules awaiting shipment to the Allied armies. It was a well-chosen target, since pack animals were the main form of transport on the Western Front; trucks carried heavier loads, but the vehicles of the time were forever breaking down. Animals were strong, needed no spare parts, and could go anywhere.

Degler organized a ring of animal poisoners from among unemployed dockworkers. His men visited corrals wherever animals were gathered for shipment, especially Norfolk, Virginia, and Van Cortlandt Park in the Bronx, New York City. As they walked along the rail fences, they jabbed the animals with long needles set in the tops of germ-filled vials. The result was that thousands of animals, already paid for by the Allies, died.

Most saboteurs, however, specialized in making and plant-ing bombs. The bombers' chief targets were Atlantic-coast seaports, particularly New York Harbor, a vast area taking in the port of New York plus Hoboken and Jersey City, New Jersey. The waterfronts of these cities were really cities within themselves, containing shipyards, railway ter-minals, warehouses, docks, and loading cranes. Here was where most of the war matériel bound for Europe was as-sembled and loaded aboard Allied merchantmen.

Several top agents were assigned to New York Harbor. Dr. Walter T. Scheele ran a bomb factory in Hoboken, where he'd set up a chemical company to cover his activities. His bombs, wicked devices made of lengths of iron pipe, were small enough to carry past guards undetected.

Scheele's men dropped their bombs into the cargo holds

and coalbins of ammunition ships shortly before sailing. A few days later, far out in the Atlantic, a timer set off the weapon, causing a small explosion and fire. To save his ship from being blown sky-high, the captain would have the area flooded with sea water. The ammunition was then landed at an Allied port, dried out, and sent to the front.

Hundreds of thousands of shells turned out to be duds, because their fuses had been ruined by the saltwater bath. In addition to the cost of useless ammunition, the Allies lost precious cargo space, the labor of dockworkers, and the countless manhours spent in hauling the cargo to the front. Most of all they lost lives when the shells failed in battle.

Robert Fay, another agent, was a one-man sabotage team. A lieutenant in the German army, Fay volunteered for sabotage work while serving in France; sabotage seemed safer than the trenches. Fay, an explosives expert, invented a bomb that attached to a ship's rudder, exploding when the rudder made a certain number of turns. He was also a champion swimmer and personally attached his devices to vessels anchored in ports along the Atlantic coast. For months the Allies couldn't figure out why munitions ships were losing their rudders in midocean. Fay was finally caught by federal agents, confessed, and received a long jail sentence. Luckily for him, the United States was still at peace; saboteurs captured in wartime were usually hung.

The worst act of sabotage in our history took place in the early hours of Sunday, July 30, 1916, at Black Tom Island. Black Tom was not really an island, but a manmade strip of land jutting into New York Harbor from Jersey City, a few hundred yards behind the Statue of Liberty. It was the most important depot in the country for loading ammunition ships. That morning thirty-four freight cars of shells, TNT, and nitroglycerine—more than two million pounds of explosives —were parked at a siding prior to loading.

A few minutes after 2:00 A.M., a terrific blast rocked the harbor. The explosion was heard a hundred miles away in Connecticut and Pennsylvania. Sheets of flame leaped skyward, making it seem from the distance that New York City itself was burning. Nearly every window in Jersey City was broken. The Statue of Liberty was riddled with shell fragments. Chunks of metal rained from the sky. Seven bodies were found in the twisted rubble.

The Black Tom saboteurs were never caught. To this day their names have never been revealed. All that is known for certain is that German agents caused the explosion, for their government agreed to pay fifty million dollars in damages after the war.

Black Tom and other outrages brought a crackdown on the spy nest in the German embassy. Captains von Papen and Boy-Ed were expelled; despite the evidence against them, their diplomatic immunity as members of the ambassador's staff saved them from arrest.

Commander von Rintelen wasn't so lucky. MI6 knew all about him from decoded messages and decided to do some mischief on its own. One day von Rintelen received top secret orders to return immediately to Berlin. Disguised, he boarded a Dutch ship in New York with a forged Swiss passport. When the vessel made a routine stop at Dover, England, security men took him away. He'd been tricked, for his "orders" came straight from London. No longer protected by diplomatic immunity in England, von Rintelen was handed over to the Americans, tried, and sent to the federal penitentiary in Atlanta, Georgia.

With the declaration of war on Germany in April 1917,

the remaining agents closed up shop and fled to Mexico. For now that we were at war, the hangman's noose, and not a jail cell, awaited them if caught.

So long as Germany kept its U-boats under control, President Wilson was willing to be patient. After all, sabotage, although a serious problem, was nowhere as serious as an all-out war.

The problem was that the Germans couldn't keep their submarines on a leash forever. The submarine was a valuable weapon, and every day Germany held it back made the Allies stronger.

A debate began in Berlin about whether or not to resume submarine warfare. The military put its case simply: either use the weapon to the fullest or risk losing the war. The diplomats answered just as simply: unleashing the U-boats would surely bring the United States into the war on the Allied side.

The kaiser's admirals and generals weren't worried. The United States, they knew, was unprepared for European-style warfare. It could never train and equip an army to make a difference in Europe. By the time the Americans were ready, the Allies would be defeated, thanks to the U-boats cutting their supply lines. The military won the debate.

On January 31, 1917, Ambassador von Bernstorff delivered a note to the State Department in Washington. The note announced that, beginning at midnight, Germany would begin "unrestricted submarine warfare." It was to be sea warfare without limit or pity. A new, wider war zone was staked out surrounding the British Isles, France, Italy, and the eastern Mediterranean. This was the zone of death. Any vessel sighted within it, warship or hospital ship, Allied or neutral, would be sunk without warning and without any attempt to rescue survivors.

Death-plunge. As their torpedoed ship sinks, men are seen pulling away in a lifeboat.

Kaiser Wilhelm II, however, had generously made a concession to the United States. One American ship a week—*one*—could sail for England if it obeyed certain rules. It had to arrive on a Sunday and leave on a Wednesday. It must be decorated appropriately: red and white stripes painted on the hull, a large flag checkered red and white displayed on each mast, an American flag flown at the stern. And, of course, the United States must promise that she carried no war matériel.

President Wilson read the message, then read it again, hardly believing his eyes. Putting the paper aside, he said in a half-whisper, "This means war."

An outcry arose the moment the note was printed in the newspapers. Spying. Sabotage. The *Lusitania*. And now this. Why, the nerve of them, said one writer, to demand that our ships be "striped like a barber's pole" and fly a rag "resembling a kitchen tablecloth." The American people were fast losing patience with Germany.

The Germans added fuel to the fire toward the end of February. British code breakers read a message from German Foreign Secretary Alfred Zimmermann to the German minister in Mexico instructing him to ask for an alliance against the United States. If the Americans came into the war, Germany promised to help Mexico conquer Texas, New Mexico, and Arizona.

The idea was silly. Mexico was in no condition to conquer anyone, not with civil war sputtering in the countryside and bandit bands roaming about freely. In March 1916, the bandit chief Francisco "Pancho" Villa raided Columbus, New Mexico, burning the town and killing sixteen people. President Wilson replied by sending General John J. Pershing after him with a small army. Although Villa escaped, the Mexican government was put on notice that it would have to prevent further raids. None occurred.

The British promptly handed over a copy of the Zimmermann message to our ambassador in London. As expected, it landed like a bombshell at home. Again, within less than a month, the American people had proof of German unfriendliness. "What next?" they wondered.

The answer came during the first two weeks of March. The *Algonquin*—American-built, American-owned, American-manned—met a submarine on the surface off the English coast. Forced to stop, she was shelled by its deck gun, while her crew scrambled to safety in the lifeboats, escaping without losing a man. A few days later, the *City of Memphis*, *Illinois*, and *Vigilancia* were torpedoed and some crewmen were killed.

That was the last straw. Grimly, President Wilson broke diplomatic relations with Germany and called Congress into special session. The man of peace would ask for a declaration of war. It was the hardest thing he'd ever have to do, but he could see no way out. Either we fought Germany or let her ride roughshod over American rights. The President had no doubt that the Senate and House of Representatives would agree to his request; indeed, they'd welcome it eagerly.

In the early evening of Monday, April 2, 1917, President Wilson set out for Capitol Hill. It was damp and dreary, a fitting evening for what he had to do, and he shuddered for a moment as he sat next to Mrs. Wilson in the big limousine.

The moment the car nosed out of the White House driveway onto Pennsylvania Avenue, a troop of cavalry surrounded the vehicle. Hooves clattered on the wet pavement, shimmering under the streetlights. The troopers spurred their mounts, making them dance to throw off the aim of any would-be assassin in the crowd.

There was plenty to fear that night. Crowds ten deep jammed the sidewalks on either side of Pennsylvania Avenue, Washington's main thoroughfare. Most people waved flags or wore red, white, and blue ribbons in buttonholes. Others, fewer but outspoken and angry, wore white armbands and chanted "No War!" There was no telling how these people might react. Senator Henry Cabot Lodge and a demonstrator had already gotten into a fistfight.

The Secret Service feared for the President's safety. It knew that the Germans had a list of Cabinet officers to be assassinated in case of war. Everyone recalled the night in July 1915, when a bomb exploded in the Senate wing of the United States Capitol. Nobody was injured then, although the blast sent chunks of jagged glass through the air and smashed down the door of the vice-president's office.

The Secret Service wasn't taking any chances tonight. As the limousine neared Capitol Hill, its passengers saw a startling sight. For the first time in history floodlights lit the white dome of the Capitol, giving the impression that it might sail into space any moment. Had the passengers looked closely, they would have seen Army and Marine sharpshooters on the rooftops; machine guns were hidden behind window curtains, positioned to sweep the street.

The rain fell harder. Lightning streaked the sky. There was the rumbling of distant thunder.

The President was shown into the chamber of the House of Representatives. The House represents the people directly, and what he had to say concerned them. The chamber was filled to capacity. Mrs. Wilson sat in the packed gallery, looking down on a sea of American flags. In addition to its own members, the seats on the House floor were occupied by the entire Senate, justices of the Supreme Court, Cabinet officers, and the diplomatic corps. Only the German diplomats were absent. They were busy at the embassy with last-minute packing and the burning of secret papers.

The audience spoke in hushed voices. Tension built as the

time of the President's arrival drew near. Some people felt as if the air in the room crackled with electricity.

At 8:32 P.M. "Uncle Joe" Cannon, Speaker of the House, announced: "The President of the United States." Cheers and applause rocked the room. Mr. Wilson walked to the rostrum, a thin figure in a black suit. You could hear a pin drop.

"Gentlemen of the Congress . . ."

The President adjusted his steel-rimmed spectacles and began to speak in firm, measured tones, his words reaching into every corner of the great room. There were no microphones then, so that he had to make his voice carry without shouting. The war message was his own, picked out word by word on his battered portable typewriter.

Calmly, sentence following sentence in logical order, he built the case against Germany. The warlords of Berlin were enemies of freedom, he said. They were warring against humanity by unleashing their U-boats to ravage the seas, blind to their victims' guilt or innocence. The United States must resist such outrages. The time for words and diplomatic sparring was past. We must fight, he said, "for the ultimate peace of the world and the liberation of its peoples. . . . The world must be made safe for democracy."

Edward D. White, the seventy-two-year-old Chief Justice of the Supreme Court, sat in the front row, his eyes fixed on the President's face. White, snowy-haired and wrinkled, was a Civil War veteran who'd never lost his fighting spirit. At these words, he tossed away his hat, leaped to his feet, and, clapping his hands above his head, gave the Rebel yell. Long ago that battlecry had chilled the blood of Bluecoats at Shiloh, Chickamauga, and countless other Civil War battle sites. Now it stirred this audience, which let go a roar like a storm. The

President Wilson: "The challenge is to all mankind. The wrongs against which we now array ourselves cut to the very root of human life."

cheers from inside the Capitol were taken up by the throngs outside, under the dripping trees.

Wilson's closing sentences were deeply emotional:

> But the right is more precious than peace, and we shall fight for the things which we have always carried nearest our hearts—for democracy, for the right of those who submit to authority to have a voice in their own governments, for the rights and liberties of small nations . . . and [to] make the world itself at last free. To such a task we can dedicate our lives and our fortunes, everything that we are and everything that we have, with the pride of those who know that the day has come when America is privileged to spend her blood . . . for the principles that gave her birth and happiness. . . . God helping her, she can do no other.

For a moment the audience hung as if suspended in midair, silent, unmoving, scarcely breathing. Then it went wild. No one there that night would ever forget the outburst of flag-waving, shouting, and foot-stomping. A wedge of Secret Service men led the President through the crowd for the ride back to the White House. All was handshakes, congratulations and happiness, as if he'd won some great victory.

Back at the White House, the Wilsons had dinner with friends. After they left and his wife went upstairs to bed, the President wandered into the empty Cabinet room. Some time later, his secretary, Joseph Tumulty, found him seated at the long table.

Wilson had just given the greatest speech of his life, yet he wasn't pleased. As they talked about the day's events, an overwhelming sadness came upon the President. Tears stood in his eyes.

"Think of what it was they were applauding," he said. "My message was a message of death for our young men. How strange it seems to applaud that."

With those words Woodrow Wilson laid his head on the table and cried.

TWO

Crossing the Big Pond

In the spring of 1917 a song by George M. Cohan, a writer of Broadway musicals, swept the Allied armies. You heard it constantly, wherever British, French, and Belgian troops were serving. They sang it in the trenches, whistled it on the march, hummed it while at camp chores. The song was called "Over There," and it told Europeans to prepare, and say a prayer, for "The Yanks are coming."

The Yanks Are Coming! Its upbeat message was a tonic, a ray of hope, promising war-weary people what they most wanted to hear. Now, for sure, they'd win. Sometime soon the Yanks would be coming over to help end this miserable war.

Actually, the United States was unprepared for full-scale warfare in the twentieth century. The regular Army of eighty thousand men was scattered around the globe in posts from home bases to Puerto Rico, Alaska, the Panama Canal Zone, the Philippines, and China. Nearly half were tied down in the Coast Artillery, manning the mammoth shore

defense guns along the Atlantic coast. Their officers had no
experience handling units of more than three or four thousand men in battle; European generals commanded upwards
of a million men.

The army of the richest nation on earth had few modern
weapons. Its fifteen hundred machine guns weren't enough
to equip a single Allied or enemy division. Its five hundred
light field guns couldn't cover three miles of the Western
Front, let alone smash through the German lines. Artillerymen had enough ammunition on hand for a nine-hour bombardment on a quiet day. We had NO heavy field artillery,
flamethrowers, or tanks. The air force was a joke.

Nobody knew these facts better than John J. Pershing,
the newly appointed commander of the AEF, the American
Expeditionary Force, which would soon be sent to Europe.
Born in 1860 in Laclade, Missouri, Pershing worked on his
father's farm and taught in a one-room schoolhouse before
entering the United States Military Academy at West Point.
After graduating at twenty-six, he was posted to commands
in the West, where he fought the Sioux and Apaches. During
the Spanish-American War, he served in Cuba with the 10th
Cavalry, an all-Negro regiment, which earned him the nickname "Black Jack." He sported that nickname for the rest
of his life and was proud of it.

"Black Jack" fit him in more ways than one. He was a
tough, hard-as-nails professional soldier. Completely fearless
himself, he admired courage in others. The highest compliment he could give anyone was to say, "He's a fighter . . . a
fighter . . . a fighter!" Strict and unsmiling, the Army rule-
book was his Bible, his law, enforced to the letter. He was
not liked, much less loved, by his men, black or white. Rather
they respected him as pupils respect a strict but just teacher.

Crossing the Rio Grande. General John J. ("Black Jack") Pershing and his staff ford the river separating the United States and Mexico in pursuit of the bandit chief Pancho Villa.

Pershing's courage and leadership ability was noticed by his superiors. One of his admirers happened to be Colonel Theodore Roosevelt of the Rough Riders; after TR became president in 1901, he "jump-promoted" Pershing from captain to brigadier general over the heads of eight hundred senior officers.

Black Jack was serving in Texas in 1915 when word came that his wife and three young daughters had died in a fire; only his son, Warren, age seven, survived. Although he remained outwardly calm, he never fully recovered from the loss of his family. Sometimes the pain in his heart showed despite his self-control. Once, when a curly-haired girl handed him a bunch of flowers, he found himself facing the welcoming crowd with tears streaming down his cheeks.

The lonely man buried himself under a mountain of Army work. The service became everything to him: career, family, home. He was the ideal choice both to lead the hunt for Pancho Villa and command the AEF.

In May 1917, Congress passed the Selective Service Act—the draft—to man the AEF. Draft boards were set up throughout the country and every man between the ages of twenty-one and thirty-one was required to register under penalty of a year in jail.

The draft was an efficient system. Men filled out forms, answered questions about themselves, and received a green card with their Selective Service number. Let's say the number was 258. That number was held by one man in each of the thousands of registration districts. Papers with the draft numbers were then placed in a glass bowl and drawn at random. If number 258 came up, everyone with it knew he'd soon receive a letter with the President's "greetings," welcoming him into the United States Army. "Your number's up" became an expression for being drafted and, later, killed in battle.

Not everyone welcomed the draft. Americans have never liked being forced to do anything, not even fighting for their country. Until the Civil War, our armies were always made up of volunteers. When the draft became necessary in 1863, riots broke out in the North. The worst riots were in New York City, where more than a thousand people died.

Although nothing like that happened during the First World War, thousands of men became draft dodgers. Police used to swoop down on ball parks, bathing beaches, and other recreation areas, demanding to see registration cards. Some tried to disqualify themselves by drinking ink, swallowing nails, or breaking their trigger fingers; one fellow gulped down a pocketwatch, hoping to make the examining doctor think he had a bad heart, or "ticker." Mountain folk in Arkansas threatened to shoot anyone who came to take them into the army.

Most draftees went willingly. The army became a melting pot, blending Americans from every walk of life. Never before had so many men from so many parts of the country come together for a single purpose. Some couldn't read, or signed their names with an X, or spoke no English. Recruits spoke fifty-one languages, including the Gaelic of ancient Ireland and Tagalog, spoken by natives of Luzon in the Philippines. German soldiers would be amazed when insulted in the accents of Berlin and Hamburg. American Indians became invaluable as radio operators. German eavesdroppers could never make sense of long messages in Sioux, Apache, or Navajo.

The first draftees were ordered to report to training camps in September 1917. The scene was much the same in small towns and big cities across the land. Going off to war was a bittersweet experience of sadness and excitement. Many had never been fifty miles from their birthplace, or slept away from home overnight. Now they found themselves marching, still in civilian clothes, to the railroad station. The high school band led the way.

The Civil War, until then our greatest conflict, linked the generations. Everyone knew its tunes. Northerners stepped out to "Marching through Georgia" and "Rally 'Round the Flag, Boys." Southerners preferred "Dixie" and "The Bonnie Blue Flag." Veterans in uniforms that had grown tighter with the years marched with the recruits, often under faded battle flags.

Draftees wait at their local station for the special train to basic training camp.

The station platform was decorated as for a party, with flags and flowers. There might be a sign with "We're Off to Kick the Kaiser!" in giant letters. Tables swayed under the weight of soda bottles, cakes, and pies, gifts from local patriotic groups.

A special train pulled in, grinding to a stop. " 'Board! All aboard!" cried the conductor.

Then there was a swirl of activity. Good-bye kisses from wives, mothers, sweethearts. Hugs and handshakes from fathers. A kid brother's watery eyes. Engine bell clanging. Last farewell. Waving. Blowing kisses. Car horns honking outside the station. Next stop, Camp So-and-So.

The government had built thirty-eight training camps, each able to hold forty thousand draftees, in various parts of the country. These were no place like home. Rows of long, low buildings, freshly painted and smelling of raw lumber, housed the camp headquarters, officers' quarters, mess hall, supply depot, hospital, and canteen. Draftees lived in two-story barracks or, in the warmer South, in canvas tents. Rain turned the freshly cleared fields to mud; dry weather meant dust storms.

From the moment you, the recruit, arrived in camp, your every waking moment became the property of Uncle Sam. The first stop was for a physical examination, which meant running around naked and being tapped, jabbed, and injected by strangers. After the physical came the barbershop, where your hair was snipped down to the roots; that way "cooties" (fleas or lice) would have nothing to hold on to.

The quartermaster's sheds came next, to draw mess kits, blankets, a bed sack to stuff with straw, and a uniform. Uniforms came in two types: uncomfortable and agonizing. The

Members of the National Guard are seen off by loved ones in Chicago on the first leg of their journey "over there."

tight-fitting blouse was made of scratchy wool of the dullest olive drab. The high, stiff collar of the jacket came up under the chin and might rub raw the neck of the overweight recruit. Trousers were like riding breeches, roomy in the seat and tapering toward the knees. The "wraps" came last, six-foot lengths of woolen bandage that were wound around each leg from knee to ankle. The trick was to have the wraps look smart without cutting off circulation in the legs. Boots came in sizes too large and too small. The outfit was crowned by a campaign hat, a high-peaked affair with a wide brim. Most draftees hoped some day to meet the designer of this uniform, alone, in a dark place.

Camp life was filled with interesting and exciting things to do. The day began with reveille at 5:30 in the morning. From then on everything was regulated by bugle call. Meals, work, training, and sick call were announced by the bugler. He was not a popular fellow.

Like soldiers before and since, you learned that "hurry up and wait" is an army tradition. You hurried to meals, only to wait outside the mess hall in the rain. You waited in line at the showers, drafty places with splintery floors, until the hot water ran out. As the men constantly shouted to each other:

> *You're in the army now,*
> *You're not behind the plow.*
> *You'll never get rich,*
> *You son of a ——,*
> *You're in the army now.*

Basic training meant learning the ABCs of soldiering. The first days of "Basic" were devoted to saluting and house-keeping. Rookies were made to understand that the survival of the Republic depended upon snapping a salute properly;

tightly made beds were equally important. Failure at these tasks brought long hours at attention in full pack or "policing the area," picking up cigarette butts and candy wrappers in the company streets. Marching and calisthenics built stamina and got recruits used to obeying orders instantly, for combat is no place to start questioning a command.

Learning combat skills was more difficult. Weapons of every kind were in short supply in the training camps. Artillerymen in some units had to practice loading and aiming on telegraph-pole cannon. Scarcity of rifles forced thousands of infantrymen to drill with wooden guns. Many a dummy marked "Kaiser Bill" had its stuffing torn out by rookies lunging with bayonets at the ends of broomsticks. Nearly half the men in certain divisions went overseas without ever having fired a rifle. Hand grenades were scarce, valuable items, not to be wasted when rocks would do just as well.

Despite the shortages, Black Jack's trainers kept the re-

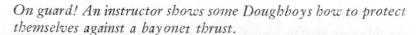

On guard! An instructor shows some Doughboys how to protect themselves against a bayonet thrust.

cruits busy every minute of the day. By the time taps blew at ten o'clock, they were too tired to notice the narrow cot with the lumpy mattress, or hear the sixty other men snoring nearby.

The trainees soon began to shape up as soldiers. They even learned a new language, soldier-talk, as colorful as any in the world. The American soldier called himself a "Yank" or "Doughboy," from "dobie" or "adobe," the white clay dust that covered marching troops during the Indian wars in the Southwest. Doughboys had their own expressions for everything. If MPs (Military Policemen) caught you going AWOL (Absent without Leave), you were SOL (Soldier Out of Luck). Your company *shavetail* (second lieutenant) might put you in the *dogeydog* (guardhouse) or assign you to KP (Kitchen Police) duty peeling a mountain of onions. Others might *goldbrick* (get out of work details) without being caught. GOK, God only knows why!

Group singing became an important part of the training routine and, later, life at the front. Officers found that singing improved morale. There were songs to go with any task, suit any mood. New recruits marched off by squads, singing "Hail, Hail, the Gang's All Here." Gripe songs helped express complaints about army life, making them easier to bear. Someone who left a good job to earn thirty dollars a month as a buck private had plenty to complain about. Corporal Irving Berlin spoke for him in the war's most famous gripe song: *Oh! How I Hate to Get Up in the Morning.*

Nasty details like digging latrines and filling sandbags became easier with rousing choruses of the nonsense song "Yaaka Hula, Hicky Dula." Songs such as "One Grasshopper Hopped Right Over Another Grasshopper's Back" made long marches seem shorter. Children at summer camp still sing this Doughboy song:

*A hundred bottles of beer on the wall, a hundred bottles
    of beer,
If one of those bottles should happen to fall, there'd be
    ninety-nine bottles of beer on the wall. . . .*

Songs, finally, built team spirit, welding strangers into a
fighting unit. Marines let go with, "We'll Hang the Damned
Old Kaiser to a Sour Apple Tree." Infantrymen roared:

*Oh, the infantry, the infantry, with the dirt behind
    their ears,
The infantry, the infantry, they don't get any beers,
The cavalry, the artillery, and the lousy engineers,
They couldn't lick the infantry in a hundred million
    years.*

The first half-million Doughboys were completing their
training by the winter of 1917. Only the "Big Pond," the
Atlantic Ocean, stood between them and France; that, and
the German U-boat fleet. Here was a task for the Navy.

The British Admiralty was keeping a secret from its own
people as well as its Allies. Germany was winning the sea
war. Ever since the start of unrestricted submarine warfare,
the monthly toll of Allied shipping had skyrocketed, reaching nine hundred thousand tons, or about one hundred vessels,
in April 1917. Once they began sinking a million tons a
month, Britain's lifeline to the outside world would be cut.
The country, which depended upon imported food, would
have to surrender or starve.
    There seemed to be no way out. Although British ship-
yards worked around the clock, ships were being sunk twice
as fast as replacements could be built. The Royal Navy's anti-

submarine efforts were also failing. Few U-boats were sunk, while the Germans launched three new vessels each week, faster models with longer cruising ranges than Schwieger's U-20.

The first American to be let in on the secret was Admiral William S. Sims. The British trusted the fifty-nine-year-old admiral as they did no other American. An expert in naval gunnery, Sims had invented the system for aiming battleship guns used in both the United States and Royal navies. He also loved Great Britain. In a speech before the war, he said that, if necessary, he believed the United States would send every man and every dollar to aid the Mother Country.

Now commander in chief of American naval forces in Europe, Sims arrived in London a few days after President Wilson's war message. He found the Admiralty shrouded in gloom. His old friend Admiral Sir John Jellicoe, chief of the Royal Navy, was clearly upset as he handed him a record of shipping losses. "It is impossible for us to go on with the war if losses like this continue," said Jellicoe. "They will win, unless we can stop these losses—and stop them soon." By "soon" he meant within six weeks.

Sims lost no time in cabling this information to Washington. The British needed ships to help with the U-boat war. Every warship fit for service must steam across the Atlantic without delay. The sea war had to be won before the land war was lost.

Sims's message set the machine in motion. Every navy yard bustled with activity, preparing vessels for distant duty. Battleships, the giants of the fleet, weighed anchor and headed east with their cruiser escorts. Five battleships—U.S.S. *New York, Wyoming, Florida, Delaware, Arkansas*—joined the Grand Fleet in the North Sea. As the Sixth Battle Squadron, they became a unit of the Royal Navy under command of a British admiral. Their mission: to prevent German surface raiders from coming out onto the open ocean. Three other battleships—U.S.S. *Nevada, Utah, Oklahoma*—took up positions at Bantry Bay, Ireland, to cover the Atlantic shipping lanes.

The most important ships, however, were the destroyers. Nicknamed "tin cans," they weighed 1,200 tons and had crews of ninety to a hundred, compared to a battleship's 29,000 tons and 2,500-man crew. Sleek and graceful, with a streamlined hull and powerful engines, the destroyer could slice through the water at express-train speed. Everything was sacrificed to speed, including protective armor plate; a hit with a big shell would split it open like a tin can, sending the flaming wreck to the bottom in seconds. The destroyer wasn't built to slug it out with the heavyweights, but to scout ahead of the fleet and hunt U-boats.

The destroyer was the submarine's natural enemy. A U-boat cruising on the surface to recharge its electrical batteries didn't have a chance against a charging destroyer. It sped to the attack with sirens screaming. Maneuvering like a boxer, it easily turned, circled, and zigzagged, throwing off the enemy's aim. Even if the U-boat fired a torpedo straight at its attacker, chances were that it did no damage. Destroyers were so light and rode so high in the water, that most torpedoes passed harmlessly under the keel.

The hunter suddenly became the hunted. The destroyer cut loose with a battery of small-caliber guns, damaging or destroying its prey. If it was near enough, it didn't have to waste ammunition. With waves slapping and wind blasting, it charged at thirty-five knots or forty miles an hour. The destroyer's bow, razor-sharp and reinforced with steel plates, could slice a U-boat in half.

A submerged U-boat was always at a disadvantage, for a destroyer could turn the U-boat's main weapon against it. A torpedo, as the *Lusitania*'s lookouts discovered, creates a bubble trail that stands out on the surface, pointing directly toward the U-boat that launched it. The destroyer simply raced down the trail to the end, then cut wide circles, first to the right, then to the left, releasing underwater bombs.

These depth charges, or ash cans, were metal barrels filled with dynamite and set to go off at different depths. The submarine, though deadly, was also fragile as an eggshell. Its hull was nothing but a thin steel envelope wrapped around engines, air tanks, work spaces, and living quarters. Even today a submarine's equipment—diving gear, navigation instruments, pressure gauges, hydroplanes—is sensitive and easily ruined.

A sailor prepares a depth charge aboard a destroyer. These 300-pound packages of explosives could cave in the hull of a submarine.

The destroyer kept circling, releasing ash cans every ten seconds. Some were rolled off its stern, others hurled to either side by Y-shaped launchers, an American invention.

A direct hit wasn't necessary. Water, unlike air, cannot be compressed, squeezed into a smaller area. Thus, an explosion within a hundred feet of a U-boat sent a stone-hard wall of water crashing against the hull. When the crew heard the sharp metallic *click* of the ash can's detonator, they braced for the blow that was sure to follow. Moments later a shock wave struck their boat with the *clang* of a sledge hammer on an anvil.

The U-boat then shook crazily, vibrating from stem to stern. Fuel lines snapped. Light bulbs shattered, plunging the vessel into darkness. Instruments went wild. The hull sprang leaks, or burst open suddenly, drowning everyone.

The destroyermen above could hear the deep-throated rumble of the depth charges, followed by a more terrible sound. A volcano of white water sprang from the sea carrying pieces of wreckage. Globs of black oil soon covered the surface. Schools of dead fish floated everywhere, killed by the depth charges' concussion.

Some U-boat commanders—the lucky ones—saved their vessels by "playing possum." If the water was shallow enough, they rested the craft on the bottom to wait out the attack; though diving deeper than three hundred feet would crush the hull under the hundreds of tons of water pressure per square inch. Commanders sometimes released oil or blew clothing and other "wreckage" from torpedo tubes to fool attackers. But even if a U-boat survived a depth-charging, crewmen were so shaken up that they were unfit for service for days afterward.

On May 4, 1917, people at the British naval base in Queens-

An American four-piper, complete with camouflage, on patrol in the North Sea. The irregular design was used to break up the vessel's silhouette, spoiling a U-boat commander's aim.

town, Ireland, saw a welcome sight. Six United States Navy "four-pipers," destroyers with four smokestacks, swept into the harbor amid a cloud of salt spray. Every vessel in the harbor hooted its whistle and broke out the American colors. Old Glory fluttered at the housetops. Schoolchildren had the day off. The newcomers were so welcome that their arrival has been known ever since as "The Return of the *Mayflower*."

These destroyers, the first of seventy-nine to go on station in European waters, were commanded by Captain Joseph K. Taussig. A spit-and-polish career officer, Taussig was anxious to get on with his assignment. So was Sir Lewis Bayly, the British admiral at Queenstown.

"Captain Taussig," he asked, "at what time will your vessels be ready for sea?"

Taussig's reply has become part of our naval folklore: "I shall be ready when fueled."

"Do you require repairs?" Bayly asked, surprised.

"No sir."

"Do you require any supplies?"

"No, sir."

"Good morning," said the admiral, turning on his heel.

The Yanks were ready, but they had a lot to learn. Most had never been in a war zone, and the first patrols were harder than they'd imagined.

The excited crews sighted more "periscopes" in a day than there were U-boats in all the navies of the world. Floating wreckage took on U-boat shapes from the distance, timbers becoming periscopes, hatch covers conning towers. Taussig's crew of the U.S.S. *Wadsworth* ran to battle stations twenty-four times in one day, probably a record for any destroyer in the Allied service. They were all false alarms.

The first submarine sighted was mistaken for a fishing boat and allowed to escape. The next submarine wasn't so lucky; the trigger-happy gunners shot it full of holes before realizing it was British. Another destroyer depth-charged a whale, killing the lumbering beast.

Antisubmarine patrol was hard, dirty, and dangerous. Hours were long, the crews working three watches, or shifts, around the clock. Since destroyers used oil as fuel, crews were covered with the greasy soot constantly pouring from the smokestacks. There was no escaping the oil gasses, which got into everything, even the food.

The seas around the British Isles, rough at the best of times, pounded the light craft. No motion in the world can compare with that of a destroyer in rough waters. It moves in three directions at once: lurching and plunging forward, rolling from side to side, and bobbing up and down like an elevator gone insane. Much of the time decks were beneath the waves. Water sloshed belowdecks, soaking into bedding and clothing. Cups and plates danced across tables. During one six-hour gale, a sailor recalled, "all hands ate off their laps, that is those who ate at all did." Most found it best to forget that they had stomachs, or needed sleep. The ship bucked and plunged so violently that it required every ounce of energy to stay in the bunks.

Yet few destroyermen asked to be transferred to quieter duty. For most, riding a tin can was the adventure of a lifetime. Excitement, the thrill of danger shared with comrades, welded the crews into large, if only temporary, families. There was never a dull moment. "Sparks," the radio operator,

A storm in the North Atlantic. Destroyermen had to get used to being on vessels that moved in three directions at once. Crewmen ate little and got practically no sleep during antisubmarine patrols.

was in constant touch with Queenstown. Messages kept crews posted about everything going on over hundreds of square miles of ocean. They might have to answer an S.O.S. call— Save Our Ship—from a torpedoed merchantman. Or perhaps a fat oil tanker was being trailed by a U-boat. There'd always be a warm glow when they recalled the cheers from a passenger liner escorted through the Irish Sea to Liverpool.

November 17, 1917, was a red-letter day for the Queenstown destroyers. The U.S.S. *Fanning* was shepherding a slow merchantman when a lookout shouted, "Periscope!"

With sirens screaming, the *Fanning* practically spun around at thirty knots and charged.

Down went the periscope.

Overboard went a string of ash cans, setting the sea boiling and churning.

Up came the U-boat. The blasts had broken her fuel lines and the captain had to decide instantly whether to go down with his vessel or spend the rest of the war in a prison camp. He chose captivity.

The submarine shot to the surface stern first, right into a hail of gunfire. Her number, U-58, was plainly visible on the conning tower, which was being stitched with machine gun bullets.

Suddenly the hatches opened and the crew came out, hands raised. *"Kamerad! Kamerad! Kamerad!"* they shouted in chorus. The Germans were calling the Yanks comrades, friends, and begging them to hold their fire.

The Americans were too surprised to notice two sailors slip below and open the submarine's sea valves; the Allies had won this round but the captain was determined to deny them this valuable prize. As U-58 slipped beneath the waves, its crew swam toward the *Fanning* and safety.

The destroyer sped toward Queenstown, her prisoners

U-58 as seen from the deck of the destroyer Fanning. *The submarine has just surfaced and the crew is begging the Americans to accept their surrender.*

warm, dry, and singing gaily, glad to be alive and out of the war. That evening the *Fanning* received a message of congratulation from Admiral Sims: "Go out and do it again!"

The destroyers also took some hard knocks from the enemy, especially at the hands of Hans Rose, skipper of U-53. Rose wasn't the typical submarine captain, who struck, killed, and fled, leaving survivors to their fate. And he certainly wasn't like those butchers who surfaced to lob a few shells into lifeboats.

One of Germany's most successful U-boat men, Rose nevertheless hated war and needless bloodshed. Whenever possible after torpedoing a ship, Rose waited around until the lifeboats were launched and filled. He'd then throw them a line to keep them together and give the victims food until destroyers steamed over the horizon. Then he'd cut the line and submerge.

On December 6, 1917, Rose upped periscope and saw a lone destroyer, the U.S.S. *Jacob Jones*, two miles away, an almost impossible target from such a distance. But luck was with him that day. A torpedo blew a hole in the vessel's starboard side and she began to sink. Most crewmen had already abandoned ship when *wham*, she was blown to bits by her own ash cans; their safety catches had been removed in preparation for battle and they went off when the sinking ship reached the proper depth. The men in the lifeboats, many of them wounded, knew they couldn't last long on the stormy Atlantic.

This time Rose didn't surface. He did something better. Deliberately giving away U-53's position by radioing Queenstown, he reported that he'd sunk one of its destroyers and where the survivors could be found. Not surprisingly, Hans Rose was the only U-boat skipper American destroyermen wanted to take alive—to shake his hand.

★

The destroyers were soon joined by the spunky little sub-chasers of the "Splinter Fleet." This nickname fit perfectly, for the subchaser, an American invention, was really a high-powered speedboat with big ears. Built of plywood, this sixty-ton, 110-foot craft could run circles around a destroyer. Its real advantage, however, wasn't speed, but its top-secret hydrophones, or "ears." These underwater listening devices had been developed by American scientists to combat the U-boats. A destroyer was effective only when a submarine gave away its position. But if it remained underwater, not firing a torpedo or showing a periscope, it was safe from the destroyer.

But not from the subchaser. Working in teams of three, the subchasers would shut off their engines and drift on the surface. Their hydrophones, lowered from beneath the vessels, were connected to wires that led to a pair of earphones worn by a sailor.

Subchaser SC-405 with the transport George Washington, *with the battleship* Pennsylvania *looking on in the background. Subchasers used sophisticated listening devices to detect submarines.*

The underwater world is anything but silent. Water is an excellent conductor, carrying sounds for many miles. The men monitoring the hydrophones learned to tell one sound from another. The barking of a whale is different from the low moan of a wreck being rolled from side to side by the currents. The rapid humming of a destroyer's propeller is unlike the slow chug, chug, chugging of a squadron of heavy warships. A school of porpoises goes *swish, swish*; so does a submarine, only at a slightly higher pitch, evident even twenty miles away.

Once the listeners had a fix, it was easy to tell the direction of the sound. Information from each subchaser was then radioed to the map room of the command vessel, where lines were drawn on a chart. The spot where the lines crossed marked the submarine's exact location. The subchasers then raced for the kill with ash cans.

Despite American help, the U-boat rampage continued unchecked. The problem was that there weren't enough antisubmarine craft to patrol the danger zones, especially around the British Isles and the French coast south of the English Channel. Each destroyer and subchaser group was assigned several "boxes," patrol areas covering hundreds of square miles of ocean. The U-boats, which had their own listening devices, had only to sit tight and wait for the hunters to move on. The Allies, said President Wilson, were "hunting hornets all over the yard," exhausting themselves without solving the problem. There had to be a better way.

That better way was found by Admiral Sims. Since arriving in England, Sims had noticed something curious. Those floating mountains, the battleships of the Grand Fleet, regularly cruised the North Sea, waters swarming with submarines. Yet, though the most tempting targets of all, they were seldom attacked and never sunk. Why?

Admiral William Sims commanded American naval forces in Europe. It was Sims who persuaded the British to adopt the convoy system to protect merchantmen from submarine attack. This photo is from 1913, when Sims was a captain in the U.S. Navy.

The explanation lay not in the vessels' own guns and armor, but in their escorts. A battle squadron was always surrounded by a double screen of cruisers and destroyers. The best a U-boat commander could hope for was to pop his periscope above the surface several miles away, have a good look at the battlewagons, and slink out of the way. Merchantmen, however, were easy targets, because they sailed alone.

Sims' keen mind saw the solution as clearly as a torpedo's wake in the water. It was a mistake to chase U-boats when they could be made to come to the hunters. Do away with individual merchant ship sailings and antisubmarine patrols. Adopt the convoy, grouping together the raiders' prey and their natural enemies. Make them fight for every merchantman. Of course there'd be losses, but Sims bet they'd be small, nothing like the nine hundred thousand tons sunk each month. In addition, the convoy would give the destroyers and subchasers the opportunity to sink U-boats in large numbers—if they dared to attack.

Admiral Jellicoe had his doubts. There weren't enough destroyers, he said, for fleet protection and convoy duty. The merchant captains wouldn't go for the idea, because it was hard to sail in formation, especially at night with the lights out. Ships would crash into each other, saving the kaiser torpedoes.

Sims insisted. President Wilson insisted. At last the Admiralty tried an experimental convoy from the Mediterranean to England in May 1917. It worked. Not a ship was sunk.

The Allies had reached the turning point in the sea war. Shipping losses tumbled by hundreds of thousands of tons each month from then on.

By the war's end, two million Doughboys had crossed the Big Pond. The Germans tried to drown them in nearly two hundred attacks on convoys. Yet only one eastbound transport, the *Tuscania*, was torpedoed with a loss of fifty-six out of the twenty-five hundred men aboard. There would be no more *Lusitanias*, now that the convoy had broken the back of the submarine offensive. Among the U-boats lost with all hands, probably when it struck a mine, was the U-88 commanded by Walther Schwieger, its new skipper.

Sailing the Atlantic in wartime was a never-to-be-forgotten experience for the Doughboys. Let's follow a typical group.

Shipping out was nothing like the hometown sendoff. The journey began on a railroad platform near one of the far-flung training camps. Troop trains were all the same, slow, cramped, and uncomfortable. Everyone grumbled, not least those who made the five-day trip up from Texas during the summer dressed in tight-fitting wool.

With few exceptions, the trains converged on one place: New York Harbor. Transports were waiting there, at the

Hoboken docks or in Brooklyn, a short ferry ride across the bay. Some Doughboys who'd never seen salt water before expected to be greeted in French at the end of the ferry ride. They had no idea of the distance between America and Europe.

The troopships were converted ocean liners unlike anything they'd imagined. No longer proud sea queens, they were "dazzle-painted" in gray, black, and white stripes and squares; the idea was to confuse U-boat commanders by breaking up the ships' normal silhouettes, making it hard to get a clear shot at their sides. Some vessels were painted the color of the ocean with another, smaller, vessel painted over them going in the opposite direction.

The ships' peacetime comforts had vanished along with their gay colors. Ballrooms and parlors had become dormitories with bunks stacked four high; men jammed into cabins on the passenger decks. A few of the larger vessels carried upward of nine thousand troops, three times their normal capacity. Living quarters were so cramped that you couldn't move around without stepping on someone. Sergeants worked overtime breaking up the fistfights that resulted. Others, however, hadn't the stomach for fighting; they were soon too seasick to get out of bed.

One by one the transports hoisted anchor, slipped down the harbor, and passed through the Narrows to the open sea. There, waiting for them, were escorts of heavy warships, cruisers, and occasionally battleships. There was little chance of attack in midocean, since the spaces were so vast that an entire fleet could easily vanish. The warships came along to ride shotgun, to drive away any German warship that might break through the blockade.

As the land faded in the distance, everyone came under

the iron law of the convoy. The ships formed groups of five or six, one behind the other, in long parallel lines. About five hundred yards separated each ship, with a mile between each line of ships. Warships patrolled the convoy's sides and rear.

Aboard each ship, nothing was left to chance. No detail, however small, was overlooked if it might alert the enemy to the convoy's course and location. The cooks' helpers were neater than they'd ever been in peacetime. Garbage, normally thrown overboard to trail behind the vessel, was sunk in weighted sacks; holes were punched in tin cans so they'd sink.

Night was a special time at sea, beautiful yet filled with hidden danger. Convoys moved in total darkness, for the tiniest speck of light might attract submarines. Somber colors made the ships invisible amid cloudbanks and swirling rain squalls. Portholes were screwed shut and painted over. And God help the Doughboy or swab (sailor) who smoked a cigarette on deck at night. He stayed belowdecks for the rest of the trip, peeling onions and doing other unpleasant tasks.

The convoy's movements, meanwhile, were being watched closely in London. The Convoy Room, a secret room beneath the Admiralty, was the nerve center of the whole system. A huge map of the Atlantic covered one wall. Tall ladders on rubber wheels allowed naval officers to reach any corner of the map. Colored threads, each with a paper boat representing a convoy, stretched from its home port—New York; Hampton Roads, Virginia; Halifax, Nova Scotia; Gibraltar; Dakar, West Africa—to a point in the ocean. As the convoy advanced, the cord was stretched and the boat moved to give its exact location. Little circles were marked in squares off the British Isles and France. These represented U-boats.

Submarine commanders were in constant touch with one another and fleet headquarters ashore. What they didn't know was that British code breakers were reading their messages, while secret radio direction finders pinpointed their location. If a U-boat seemed too close for comfort, London radioed the convoy to shift course out of harm's way.

Nearing Europe, the convoy entered the danger zone, the U-boats' favorite killing grounds. Shipboard security became stricter than ever. Lifeboat drills were held constantly; life preservers were worn all the time, even while asleep. The lead vessel hoisted a signal flag and the entire convoy began to zigzag as one. Zigzagging, a series of sharp turns to right and left, spoiled a submarine commander's aim.

One morning, as the sun rose, the Doughboys noticed that the big warships were gone. They had turned around, returning to port to pick up a new convoy. From the mist, bursting through the swells, came destroyers and subchasers to escort them through the death zone. Like frisky sheepdogs, they wove in and out among the lumbering transports, looking for trouble. Some blew smoke, laid smoke screens to hide the convoy.

The destroyermen could feel the anxiety aboard the crowded transports. Captain William F. Halsey—Admiral "Bull" Halsey of World War II fame—wrote in his diary about meeting a Doughboy convoy: "You look at them and pity them having to go in the trenches. [I] suppose they look at us and wonder why anyone is damn fool enough to roll and jump around in a destroyer."

On June 27, 1917, early risers in the French seaside town of St. Nazaire awoke to find that strange ships had arrived during the night. A bugler aboard one ship began to play. The notes of "The Star-Spangled Banner" drifted across the water, cold and metallic in the balmy summer air. Fourteen thousand men, the advance guard of the First Division of the Regular Army, known as "The Big Red One" from its shoulder patch, landed that afternoon together with a regiment of United States Marines.

It was the leading edge of a human tidal wave that would soon surge across the Atlantic.

The Yanks had come.

The first American troop transport to arrive at St. Nazaire in June, 1917.

THREE

"Lafayette, We Are Here!"

★ July 4, 1917. On this day a battalion of the 16th Infantry Regiment, First Division, set out on a march through the streets of Paris. It seemed that everyone in the City of Light had turned out along their route, overflowing the sidewalks and leaving only a narrow lane for the marchers.

The day belonged to the men from across the ocean. Bands, in a good imitation of a broken record, played "The Star-Spangled Banner" nonstop. Old Glory flew from the buildings, draped automobiles, adorned buttonholes; it even decorated horses' bridles.

As the column threaded its way through the crowds, its progress was marked by waves of shouting: *"Vivent les Américains," "Vive Pershing," "Vivent les États Unis."* Long live the Americans. Long live Pershing. Long live the United States.

Blizzards of colored paper fell from the rooftops. Women, many in black widow's weeds, stood on the sidelines, weeping. Old graybeards bared their heads as the marchers went

by. Young women forced their way into the ranks, swinging along arm-in-arm with the Doughboys. Pretty girls kissed their cheeks, or blew kisses from the distance. The column came to look more like a moving flower garden than a military formation. Soldiers marched with wreaths around their necks, flower petals covering their campaign hats, and single stems poking out of their rifle barrels.

At last the column reached its destination, Picpus Cemetery, resting place of so many French heroes. As the Doughboys stood at attention, Black Jack Pershing and his staff walked to the marble tomb of the Marquis de Lafayette. Pershing placed a wreath of pink and white roses on the tomb, mumbled a few words in halting French, and stepped back. Captain Charles Stanton, his friend, now stepped forward. Groping for words, Stanton snapped a salute and cried: *"Nous voilà, Lafayette!"* "Lafayette, we are here!"

"Lafayette, we are here!" Men of the First Division march through Paris on their way to the tomb of the Marquis de Lafayette, Independence Day, 1917.

Lafayette went to the United States to help us win our independence during the American Revolution. We were about to repay the favor by helping to drive an invader from French soil.

The holiday mood that day was genuine; the cheers and tears came from the heart. The Doughboys were the Allies' last hope of winning the war.

Thus far, 1917 had been a bad year for the Allies. In the early spring, revolution had broken out in Russia, followed by a civil war in which Communists under V. I. Lenin overthrew the government. In April, only days after Congress

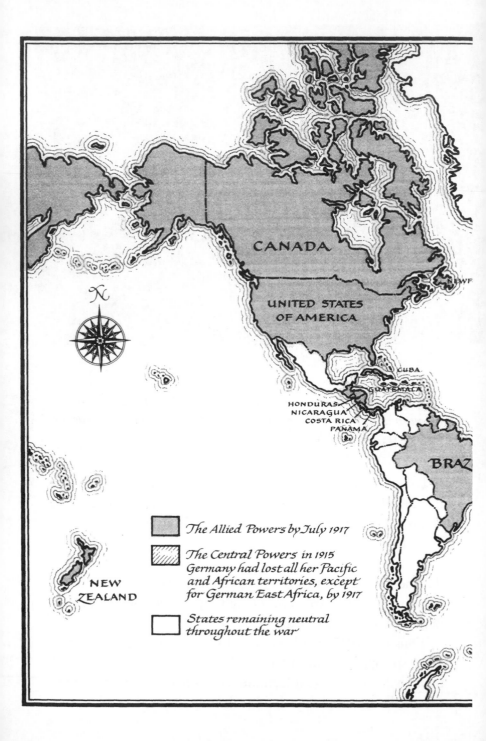

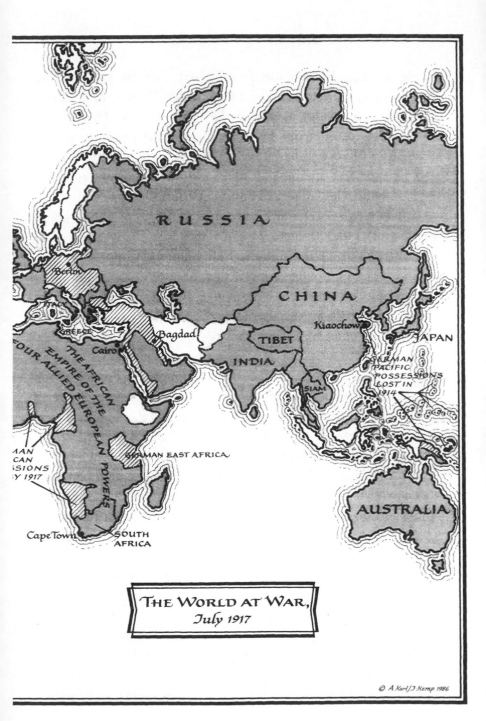

RUSSIA

CHINA

Berlin

ITALY

GREECE

Cairo

Bagdad

TIBET

INDIA

Kiaochow

JAPAN

GERMAN PACIFIC POSSESSIONS LOST IN 1914

THE AFRICAN EMPIRE OF THE FOUR ALLIED EUROPEAN POWERS

SIAM

...MAN ...CAN ...SIONS ...Y 1917

GERMAN EAST AFRICA

AUSTRALIA

Cape Town

SOUTH AFRICA

THE WORLD AT WAR,
July 1917

© A. Karl / J. Kemp 1986

declared war, French General Robert Nivelle launched a massive assault to regain the Chemin des Dames, or Ladies' Road, a key ridge overlooking the French lines. The offensive was crushed by German artillery and machine guns, costing Nivelle 120,000 men in five days. The British fared still worse. Late in July they began an all-out attack at Passchendaele Ridge in Belgium. When the attack ground to a halt weeks later, they had gained fifty square miles—at a cost of 340,000 men. During the fall the Germans and Austrians broke through the Italian lines at Caporetto, killing and wounding 600,000 men.

These setbacks nearly destroyed Allied morale, their fighting spirit. British troops, among the finest in the world, sometimes marched to battle braying like sheep. *Baaa. Baaa. Baaa.* Such pitiful cries were meant to show that they felt like helpless animals being led to the slaughter. French troops mutinied. During May and June, tens of thousands of French *poilus* (literally "hairy ones") refused to fight or take orders; the war must end, they insisted, even if the Allies lost. Although the mutinies were kept secret from the French people, and the mutineers' leaders were executed, the high command knew that the situation was desperate. The Allies, nearing exhaustion, pinned their hopes on the vast armies forming in America.

Yet their hopes couldn't be realized any time soon. Although the convoys brought Yanks in ever-growing numbers, they were unprepared for battle. Supplies weren't ready. Nor were the Doughboys, who had a lot more to learn about fighting than they'd been taught in basic training.

Napoleon, France's greatest soldier, said, "An army marches on its stomach." It does; and the larger the army, the bigger the stomach. For the bravest soldier is helpless without food and ammunition to feed his weapons. And a soldier without proper clothing is in line for the hospital, or the burying ground.

Experts in logistics, the science of supplying armies in war, estimated that a combat soldier needed at least sixty pounds of supplies and equipment each day, every day. From then on it was a matter of simple arithmetic. An American infantry division of the First World War had 29,000 officers and men, needing 1,740,000 pounds of supplies; that's 174 five-ton carloads each day.

To get the job done, Pershing created the Services of Supply (SOS), a behind-the-lines army equal in size to the forces at the front. SOS, whose motto was "We deliver the goods," required enormous facilities to unload, handle, store, and transport supplies. Yet few of these facilities existed when the AEF began to arrive in France. As a result, ports along the Atlantic—Bordeaux, Pauilac, la Pallice, St. Nazaire, Brest—were invaded by the United States Army Engineers. Pile drivers sank foundations for docks able to handle dozens of merchantmen at once. Tens of thousands of stevedores were put to work unloading the ships.

Many of these stevedores were blacks from the levees of the Mississippi. They dressed differently from their fellow Doughboys. When America entered the war, there was a shortage of olive drab for uniforms. A supply officer located a warehouse in Washington full of uniforms wrapped in newspapers dated 1865. These were the old blue uniforms of the Union Army, packed away after the Civil War. Once worn by men who fought to rid America of slavery, these uniforms were now worn by the sons and grandsons of these freed slaves.

Unloaded supplies were stored in a warehouse complex

large enough to service the AEF for a month. A typical order might be for three days' supplies for 350,000 men: 1,250,000 cans of tomatoes, 1,000,000 pounds of sugar, 600,000 cans of corned beef, 750,000 pounds of canned hash, 150,000 pounds of dried beans. The order, received in the morning, was on its way by sunset.

Supplies were transported over hundreds of miles of new railroad track. Locomotives, eleven hundred of them, plus uncounted freight cars, were shipped flat and reassembled by a special railroad engineering regiment. Trains pulled into depots behind the front, where the supplies were transferred to trucks, pack mules, and horse-drawn wagons for delivery to the troops. The animals were cared for by the ten-thousand-man Army Veterinary Service. SOS, finally, saw to it that nothing was wasted, if possible. Worn uniforms, underwear, coats, belts, and boots were repaired and reissued. Battlefield junk might be collected and returned to the enemy as shrapnel, artillery shells filled with scrap metal. SOS repair shops handled anything from cannon and motorcycles to sewing machines and machine guns.

No sooner did a convoy arrive, than the Doughboys were hustled into freight cars marked "*Chevaux*-8, *Hommes*-40," eight horses or forty men. The cars smelled of horse sweat and manure; odd lumps of manure remained in the darkened corners. The smell got into everything during the next two days and nights; into the straw they slept on, into the food they ate, into their clothes and hair. Their destination was the Vosges, a low range of mountains in east-central France near the Swiss border, an hour's drive from the war zone. Here they would complete their training, learning to fight and survive on the Western Front.

Waste not, want not. Shoes worn out by soldiers at the front are collected at a salvage depot to be repaired and reused.

The training itself became a struggle for survival. Living conditions were deliberately made difficult to prepare them for the trenches. The Doughboys lived, not in barracks, but in barns, stables, haylofts, and unused buildings in the villages that dotted the countryside. Their quarters, damp and stinking, were impossible to keep clean. The food was awful. Lunch, the day's main meal, might consist of a strip of fatty bacon, a couple of hardtack biscuits, a boiled potato, and a mugful of weak coffee. "Captain," a Doughboy said, "I'd just like to get my head in a Camp Hancock garbage can for thirty minutes and get a square meal."

At first villagers and their guests were puzzled by one

"Horses, 8; Men, 40." Members of the Fifth Marine Regiment crowd into a freight car on the way to training camps in the Vosges region of France.

another. Both peoples seemed so strange, like natives of different planets. The Doughboys, many of whom had never heard a language other than English, wrestled with French. The French were amazed at the Doughboys. Their mouths always seemed to be full of a rubbery glob called gum. Frenchmen watched, disbelieving, as Yanks bathed in streams every day, in all kinds of weather; European country folk seldom bathed more than once a week.

Strangeness soon gave way to affection. The Yanks, generous and kindhearted, made friends easily. They were like overgrown boy scouts. It was common to see an off-duty soldier draw water or carry firewood for an aged peasant. But the village children were their greatest fans. At Christmas 1917, Doughboys, remembering other youngsters far away, collected money for gifts. Then a Doughboy *Père Nöel* (Father Christmas) passed out toys, candy, and clothing. Whatever differences still remained vanished like ice in summer. The mayor of one town spoke for everybody: "Never, perhaps, have such bonds been obtained between two nations . . . [Christmas] was, indeed, a feast of two great families."

In the meantime, Yanks studied war with experts, the 47th Division, taken from the front to serve as instructors. Known as the "Blue Devils" from their light blue uniforms and helmets, they were the best troops in the French army. Tough as piano wire, each was a veteran of countless battles. Now they'd teach their new friends all the lessons they'd learned so painfully themselves.

The Blue Devils quickly earned their pupils' respect. On forced marches over rugged terrain, weighed down by fifty-pound packs, they could walk the legs off the strongest Doughboy. They thought nothing of picking up a rifle by the bayonet tip with two fingers. A favorite trick was to juggle three hand grenades, nasty things with a habit of exploding if bumped the wrong way.

Apart from their own rifles and pistols, Americans fought the First World War with borrowed equipment. Steel helmets, even thousands of uniforms complete with brass buttons bearing the monogram of King George V, came from England. France contributed nearly all their grenades, machine guns, tanks, flamethrowers, light and heavy artillery. Automatic rifles were French Chauchats, the famous Sho-Sho or Sure-shot, said to be made of rusty sardine cans.

The Blue Devils put the Americans through their paces until they could take a weapon apart, clean it, and reassemble it blindfolded; weapons, after all, don't get dirty or jam only in daylight.

Trench warfare was made as realistic as possible, without actually killing the other team. Blue Devils and Doughboys would start digging toward each other from opposite ends of a field, singing as they worked. The Yanks let go with a new song, soon to become the favorite of the AEF: "Mademoiselle from Armentières." There were countless verses about this mysterious lady:

> *Oh, Mademoiselle from Armentières, parley-vous?*
> *Oh, Mademoiselle from Armentières, parley-vous?*
> *Oh, Mademoiselle from Armentières,*
> *She hasn't been kissed in forty years,*
> *Hinky dinky, parley-vous?*

When the diggers met, the team that dug the least was given a few extra hours of practice.

There was no more drilling with wooden guns. The Doughboys fired live ammunition, and they fired it often. As heavy machine guns fired five hundred bullets a minute

Goodbye to friends young and old. French children wave to Doughboys going off to the front.

over their heads, they wriggled under barbed wire entanglements. Sometimes men died during these exercises.

Training was hard, but it also hardened the Doughboys. Veterans would later look back on these days in the Vosges with gratitude. "It was this period that made us tough," said one. "We got tough, and stayed tough. When we went into the trenches, we were so mean that we would have fought our grandmothers."

As each unit completed its training, it was sent to the front. Its first assignments were in quiet sectors to get used to being near the enemy. Not every part of the Western Front was an active battlefield. Certain sectors seldom saw fighting because they were out-of-the-way or of small value. Both sides in these regions had a gentleman's agreement to live and let live. Trenches here were deep and well-drained, about as comfortable as trenches can be. If patrols met in the night, the men kept moving, pretending the other fellows didn't exist. Bombardments always came at the same time each day to give the enemy time to take cover. Often even that was unnecessary, the shells being carefully aimed to land in empty fields. Soldiers in quiet sectors tried to make the best out of the worst of wars. Then the Americans arrived.

The Doughboys saw things differently. As newcomers to war, they had none of the caution of European veterans, who knew what it was all about. War was a novelty to them, an exciting game with deadly toys. They hadn't learned, *yet*, to appreciate the fighting skills of the German soldier. He was still only half-real, a funny nickname: Kraut, Hun, Jerry, Fritzie, Heinie. Whatever his name, they'd come a long way to fight him and, by thunder, they would.

Yanks brushed aside friendly warnings to keep things quiet. They began to take potshots at enemy sentries and pitch grenades at his outposts. Gunners developed an annoying habit of sending shells close to headquarters dugouts. Jerry decided to teach these brash *Amerikaner* a lesson.

At nightfall on November 2, 1917, a two-hundred-fifty-man company of *Stosstruppen* (Storm Troopers), the German version of the Blue Devils, filed into the trenches near Barthelement. Opposite were men of the 16th Infantry, the same who'd marched to Lafayette's tomb. At 3:00 A.M. gunflashes lit the eastern sky. Tons of high explosives plunged earthward, sending fountains of earth and stone leaping skyward.

"Barrage!" men shouted, startled awake.

The shells fell in the pattern of a hollow square or box. The box crept forward slowly, deliberately, searching for its objective. At last it fell around a platoon of Doughboys, fifty-eight men, isolating them within walls of death. Nobody could escape; nobody could come to their aid.

Suddenly the explosions on one side of the box stopped, revealing gray-uniformed men with helmets that came down over their ears and neck, their faces blackened with burnt cork. Storm Troopers.

The Germans were amazed at their reception. Instead of panicking as they'd expected, the outnumbered Doughboys fought back with everything that came to hand—rifles, grenades, knives, chunks of wood, fists. The enemy was finally able to take eleven prisoners, withdrawing as the box closed behind them and rolled back across the field. Then all became quiet.

Three Doughboys lay dead in their trench: Corporal James B. Gresham, Private Thomas F. Enright, Private Merle D. Hay. They were the first American soldiers ever killed in combat in Europe; the first of many.

By the spring of 1918, Americans were taking up positions along more active sections of the Western Front, gradually settling into the routine of trench life. The trenches completed their education, for it was there that they finally learned what President Wilson had known all along: there is no glory in war, only waste and misery. Before turning to their battles, we must see how they lived.

The Doughboys' training, even a tour of duty in the quiet sectors, gave only the slightest idea of what to expect in the fighting lines. Whenever possible, troops moved up to the front at night. Life above ground was always dangerous in daylight even five to ten miles behind the lines. Enemy spotter planes were constantly darting across to pinpoint targets for the artillery. Anything that moved became a target, including ambulances bringing wounded to field hospitals. Gunners often fired blindly, hoping for a lucky hit.

Troops set out on foot, each carrying an overloaded backpack containing not only his own things but extra tools and weapons. The pack never weighed less than fifty pounds, and sometimes weighed twice as much. The average Doughboy carried:

heavy overcoat	woolen cap
shirts	waterproof groundsheet
sweater	blanket
socks	bandages
comb	gas mask
toothbrush	rifle, rifle cover, bayonet, pistol
mess kit	150–200 rounds of ammunition
shaving supplies	hand grenades
canteen	shovel
towel	extra boots

In addition to his regulation gear, the soldier carried personal things such as writing equipment, letters, and pictures of loved ones. A two-pound helmet pressed down on his skull.

Approaching the front at night was an eerie experience. Each man walked in silence, wrapped in his own thoughts. The hulks of gutted buildings, all that remained of once-beautiful towns, cast ghostly shadows in the moonlight. Here and there were the skeletons of burned-out trucks. Freshly dug graves were reminders that this was for real. And always

A Doughboy displays his field equipment, which never weighed less than fifty pounds. The outfit shown here, though heavy, is incomplete, lacking steel helmet and gas mask.

there was the distant flash and rumble of the guns.

Their destination, the trenches, were not merely long slits cut into the ground. Designed by military engineers, the trenches were supposed to protect soldiers during enemy attacks. They were never straight for more than a few yards; for if enemy raiders leaped into a trench, they could set up a machine gun to fire down its length, killing everyone. To prevent this, a trench was built with wiggles that broke it into smaller sections, each separated by a traverse, an earthen wall jutting into it from the side. The straight sections, or firebays, were reinforced with sandbags and had a low sandbag wall, or parapet, in front. Men stood in the firebays, ready at any moment to beat off an attack.

Trenches were built in at least three rows, one behind the other, to halt the enemy's advance if he broke through the first line. You traveled from one trench line to another underground through zigzagging communications trenches.

The frontline trench was the most important. Jutting out from it at right angles were narrow passages about sixty feet long leading to the saps. A sap was a listening post where three sentries peered into the blackness, straining for the slightest sign of enemy activity. Duty in a sap meant almost certain death if the enemy attacked during your shift.

Beyond the saps were row upon row of wire entanglements meant to slow an attacker's advance. Different kinds of wire, all nasty, were attached to wooden frames or to stakes driven into the ground. Some wire had barbs thick as a man's finger that cut deeply and held tightly in a wound, pinning its victim like a fish at the end of a hook. Razor wire was just that: strands with extra-heavy razor blades hooked on each end. The wire was often rusty, so that the slightest scratch might cause blood poisoning. Empty tin cans dangled

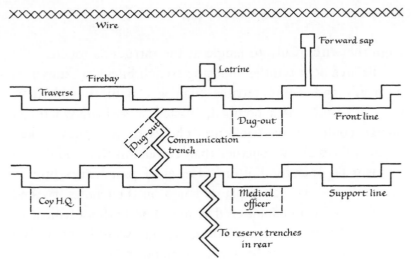

FRONT LINE TRENCHES

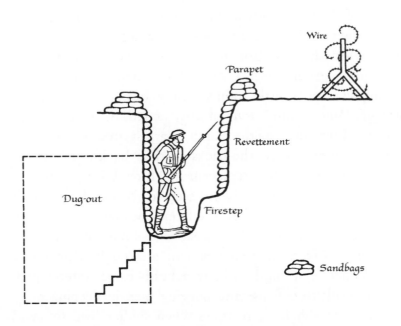

SIDE-VIEW OF TRENCH

from the wire, ready to jangle at the intruder's touch.

The area between the opposing trench lines was known as no-man's-land. More terrible than any natural wilderness, no-man's-land was a bombed, blasted wasteland where no human could survive for long. The earth was pockmarked by shell holes closer together than craters on the moon, with stagnant pools at the bottom. Traces of past battles littered the landscape. Wrecked planes stood on their noses, twisted masses of wire and splintered wood. The bodies of men, or pieces of bodies, lay everywhere; no one would risk his life to bring back a corpse for burial from no-man's-land.

Life in the trenches was an endless round of suffering, fear, and death. War is never pretty, but trench warfare was ugliest of all. There were no beds, let alone sheets and pillows. A common soldier simply scooped out a hollow in the trench wall, where he slept for an hour or two wrapped in his waterproof groundsheet. Officers fared little better, sleeping in dugouts, stuffy little rooms used as headquarters and for storage. When a unit's tour of duty ended, the men were so exhausted that they might march to a rest area asleep. They were too numb to feel the packs on their backs, or hear the shells dropping on their replacements. Nor did they care.

When it rained, as it always seemed to do when a fresh unit went into the trenches, the front became a sea of mud. This mud was a thick, deep paste that could suck a man's boots off his feet. Each step became a struggle, demanding every ounce of strength. The trenches became waterlogged, causing walls to collapse and burying men in sleeping holes and dugouts. There were times when soldiers had to stand for days up to their chests in cold, oozing mud. The wounded often drowned in it, disappearing before rescuers could find them.

A quiet moment. American troops having a meal in their trench in the front lines, March, 1918. The bundles of wood in the left foreground were used to support the trench walls, preventing cave-ins when it rained.

Men survived in the trenches, always wet, always cold, always dirty. Soap was useless, because clean water was too precious to use for washing.

The Doughboy was the best-fed soldier of the First World War, although you'd never know it from his letters and songs. He had more food than any of his Allied comrades; he ate like a prince, compared to Jerry, who had to get by on horsemeat and dried vegetables.

Army rations were dull, tasteless, and usually cold. Hot meals were a luxury at the front, as smoke from field kitchens was an invitation to enemy artillerymen. Most of the time the Doughboy's nourishment came from "iron rations"—out of a can. He was fed canned meat said to be beef, but which everyone called "monkey meat"; it was stringy, fatty, and didn't smell very appetizing. Other iron rations were "goldfish," a cheap grade of salmon, more bone than fish, and "Corned Willie," corned beef. These were eaten with hardtack, which looked like dog biscuit and tasted about the same.

Whenever possible, soldiers preferred dishes of their own invention. A wild rabbit or a farmer's stray cow went into the pot for "slumgullion"—soldier stew. One delicacy was the trench doughnut, a crust of stale bread fried in bacon fat and covered with sugar. Water-cooled machine guns provided a quickie treat. Machine gunners fired off a few thousand bullets just to get the water boiling, then drained it into a mug with some tea leaves.

Doughboys shared their trenches with two other hungry creatures. The first was the body louse, or "cootie." These tiny creatures resembled hairy crabs and came in every color of the rainbow. Completely democratic, they attacked anyone from private to general, the clean and the dirty. Once cooties adopted a soldier, they set up permanent housekeeping on his skin and in the folds of his uniform. He gave them everything they needed: shelter, warmth, food, a place to lay their eggs. You might see whole companies of Doughboys squirming in their tight uniforms, scratching their heads for dear life. Rest periods were spent in "reading your shirt," carefully going over the seams to pick out the insects one by one.

Nobody sang about the trench rats. These creatures, with their pointy snouts and blazing eyes, swarmed at the front in millions. Scurrying and tumbling over each other, they grew enormous on the garbage that littered the trenches and on the unburied bodies in no-man's-land. Their screeching and chattering were as constant as the guns, adding to the terror of the night. Altogether fearless, they scrambled over the faces of sleeping men, or burrowed into their packs and pockets for food. A wounded man in a shell hole had more to fear from them than from his wounds. He fought to stay conscious, knowing that he'd never awaken if he passed out. Rats could strip a body to the skeleton.

Words cannot fully recreate the odor of the trenches. They stank, a sickening mixture of foul things stirred together: mud, sweat, corpses, unwashed feet, manure, garbage, rotting vegetation. The stench often became so bad that soldiers demanded an extra tobacco ration to mask it awhile.

Danger lurked everywhere, always. No-man's-land and the trenches beyond were deceptively peaceful. Nothing stirred. Nobody was visible. Yet watchful eyes constantly scanned the opposing positions.

Reading your shirt. Two Doughboys take time out to hunt cooties and body lice, in the seams of a shirt. These insects made soldiers miserable, although not as miserable as the rats that infested the trenches.

Some eyes peered through small periscopes, anxious to detect any movement that might signal an attack. Other eyes, snipers' eyes, were glued to the telescopic sights of high-powered rifles. Snipers were calm, patient men who seldom missed. An enemy soldier had only to pop his head over the parapet for an instant, or pass behind a gap in the sandbags, and *bang!* He fell dead with a bullet in the brain, shot by an invisible marksman a half-mile away.

An artillery bombardment was the most terrible experience of all. The numbers of shells fired during the First World War are almost impossible to imagine. The British alone shot off over 170 million—over five million tons of high explosives. During one day in September 1917, their gunners used a million shells of various sizes.

Most shells were fired by the field artillery, guns able to throw a fifteen-pound whizbang (a small low-traveling shell) seven miles. There were also mammoth cannon as large as any on a battleship. Able to fire a one-ton shell ten miles, these guns were so large that each needed its own railroad train. A gun train had a powerful locomotive, ammunition cars, and quarters for the crew. The gun itself was mounted on a flatcar reinforced with lengths of railroad track. Its shells, taller than a man, had to be loaded by a crane.

No thunderstorm can compare to a full-scale bombardment. Flashes of man-made lightning lit the sky. The shells' noise could be felt as well as heard. The wind as they roared overhead seemed to one soldier like "a solid ceiling of sound."

As the bombardment reached its peak, shells landed near (or in) the defenders' positions at the rate of twenty to thirty a minute. Tall trees crashed down as if snapped by a mighty axe. Domes of earth the size of a barn rose into the air, then settled with a heart-stopping thud. Jagged shell fragments zinged overhead. Slivers of stone traveled with bullet speed.

Men huddled in trenches and dugouts, feeling helpless and small. Nothing they did, or didn't do, seemed to make a difference. Chance alone decided life and death. A Dough-boy standing on a firestep survived overhead shellbursts with-out a scratch, while comrades nearby were buried alive by a direct hit on their dugout, a deep shelter roofed with four feet of logs and stone. Men vanished in a splash of crimson. Others walked away after being tossed naked a dozen yards, blown out of their clothes by a shell's concussion.

A battleship-sized railroad gun firing on targets over twenty miles away.

To sit out a bombardment was to live a nightmare. Strong men lost their self-control as the tension mounted. Moaning or whimpering like that of frightened animals came from the trenches. Entire companies began to cry, while nearby others shouted at the top of their voices to drown out the shells.

Suddenly sirens blared from observation posts in the rear, their shrill alarm rising above the explosions. The enemy was sending over poison gas.

A poison gas attack as seen from the air. Notice how the wind drives the gas cloud forward, while everything behind the gas cylinders is clear.

Early in this century chemists found that certain liquids turn to deadly gasses when released into the air. Never before or since the First World War has poison gas been used so widely. During the Second World War the Japanese used it sometimes in China; Hitler's Nazis killed millions of Jews in gas chambers. But it was not used on Europe's battlefields or in the savage island campaigns of the Pacific.

The First World War was different. Every major battle between 1915, when Germany began gas warfare, and the end of the war three years later saw this terror weapon used by both sides, including the Americans, who built the world's largest gas-producing factories.

Soldiers who'd never been exposed to gas in combat might easily ignore it, especially at night, when it became almost invisible. Its odor was a lot better than the ordinary smells of the trenches. Chlorine gas had a light green color and was like a mixture of pineapple and pepper. Doughboys compared the brownish-yellowish mustard gas to perfumed soap, garlic, or mustard. The same guns that sent over high explosives also fired gas shells, which landed with a dull *plop*; gas was also released from containers planted in the ground downwind of the enemy.

The only protection against gas was to keep your body covered and to wear a gas mask, a heavy, uncomfortable contraption of black rubber and containing chemicals to purify the air you breathed. There were also oversized masks for horses and mules, who lived through the same ordeal as their masters.

Anyone caught unprotected in a gas attack was a goner. Exposed skin became blistered, quickly turning into a mass of oozing ulcers. Gas in the eyes caused blindness, temporary or permanent, along with unbearable pain. Inhaling gas

meant slow death by suffocation; victims' faces turned purple
as they struggled for each breath until they could struggle no
more. The AEF alone suffered seventy thousand gas casualties, over one-quarter of its total casualties during the war.

Sooner or later the bombardment stopped. The silence was
so strange that troops thought for a moment that they'd gone
deaf. Yet the silence marked not the end, but the beginning
of their troubles. For the lifting of a barrage meant that
enemy assault troops had gone "over the top." They had
leaped over the parapet of their own trenches and were racing across no-man's-land. The shelling had stopped so as not
to fall on the advancing troops.

The defenders' artillery now began to tune up. Thousands

*British soldiers blinded by poison gas during Ludendorff's spring
1918 offensive wait for medical attention. They hold into each
other's shoulders while an unwounded soldier leads the way.*

of gas shells exploded over no-man's-land, blanketing it in thick clouds of poison. Explosions ripped through the advancing troops. Singly and in fives, tens, and twenties, men toppled over.

The survivors kept coming, stepping over the dead, ignoring the cries of the wounded. As they approached the sandbagged parapet, machine guns began chattering from along the trench line, each spitting five hundred slugs a minute. Men went down in neat, even rows.

At last the attackers reached the barbed wire. Some entanglements had already been blown away by the shelling, so they passed through easily. Elsewhere engineers cleared pathways with Bangalore torpedoes, lengths of pipe filled with dynamite. All the while riflemen fired at them from the trenches as fast as they could load their weapons.

Attackers were usually driven back before reaching the barbed wire. If not, they leaped into the trench with bloodcurdling war cries. The battle now became a hand-to-hand brawl with men fighting singly or in small groups. Each sap, each firebay, became a battleground with pistols, knives, and grenades as the chief weapons. Soldiers also had their own inventions for close-in fighting. Trench clubs were heavy pieces of wood studded with nails. Short-handled spades were sharpened and used as combination swords and battle axes; a single blow with this weapon could cut off a man's head or lop off an arm.

If the attackers succeeded, all they had to show for their efforts was a corpse-filled trench; they couldn't advance further, because the support trenches were still strongly defended and they were exhausted. If they failed, all anyone had to show was lots of dead and wounded.

The sufferings of the wounded continued long after the battle. The First World War happened before the age of

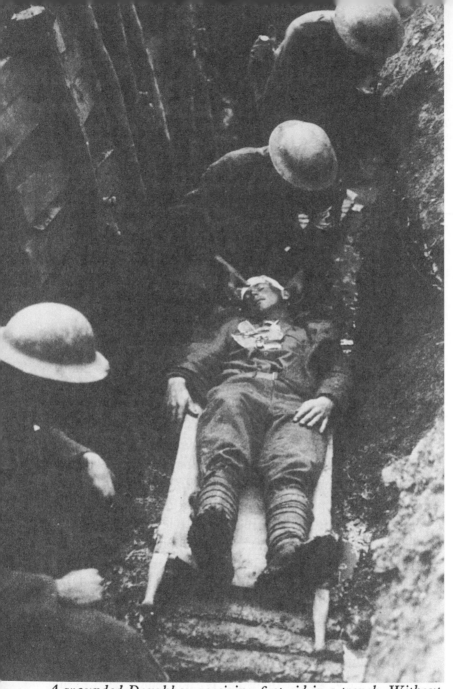

A wounded Doughboy receiving first aid in a trench. Without antibiotics, First World War soldiers were in constant danger of infection even from the slightest wounds.

miracle drugs. Although there were disinfectants to clean wounds, there were no antibiotics, such as penicillin, to prevent or treat infection. Thus thousands died who could easily have been saved today. We know of men who had an arm amputated because they scratched a finger on rusty barbed wire.

There was only one painkiller, and this always caused trouble. Morphine, a powerful narcotic made from the opium poppy, relieved pain but made the patient addicted after a few injections. No sooner did his wounds begin to heal, than he had to fight morphine addiction. Yet few lost their private battle. Doughboys were strong-willed men, nearly all of whom forced their bodies to become drug-free after weeks of suffering.

Certain wounds couldn't be bandaged or treated with drugs. The heavy bombardments helped create a new disease. There is a limit to everything. A person can take only so much noise, escape only so many near misses, before becoming shell shocked. Like terrified zombies, shell shock victims stared blankly into space with glazed eyes, their bodies trembling uncontrollably. It could happen to anyone, coward or hero, and so carried no shame for the victim. The only treatment was plenty of quiet, rest, and tender care away from the thundering of the guns.

Life on the Western Front was nasty—and about to become a lot nastier for the Doughboys. As winter's snow melted and spring's first blossoms poked their heads through the broken sod of no-man's-land, the enemy completed plans for his last campaign of the war. This time he meant to win, whatever the cost.

It promised to be an eventful year, 1918, the year Pershing's AEF faced its supreme ordeal.

FOUR

Trial by Fire

★ On a cold day early in 1918, General Erich Ludendorff, commander of German armies on the Western Front, sat at his desk deep in thought. Ludendorff, fifty-two, was a tall, heavyset man with a pudgy face, close-cropped hair, and a bristling mustache. The monocle squeezed in front of his right eye made his face appear frozen into a frown.

He *was* gloomy. Unsmiling and harsh, he made everyone uncomfortable, including his own family.

Ludendorff had plenty to think about this morning. Time was running out for his country. Secret reports showed that convoys were bringing tens of thousands of Doughboys to France each month. There was no way to stop or slow down their arrival; indeed, he expected (correctly) to be facing over a million Yanks by year's end. The Americans couldn't win the war by themselves. But they could tip the odds against Germany, already outnumbered along the Western Front, making defeat certain.

Yet the cloud might still have a silver lining. There was good news from Russia, where Lenin's Communists were in

General Erich Ludendorff, thinking. As commander of German armies on the Western Front, Ludendorff gambled everything on a series of massive assaults in the spring of 1918.

power. Having overthrown the government, they found themselves in the midst of a brutal civil war. Reds (Communists) and Whites (people loyal to Czar Nicholas II) slaughtered each other without mercy. Unable to fight their fellow Russians *and* Germany at the same time, the Communists decided to get out of the war. On December 2, 1917, they signed the Treaty of Brest-Litovsk surrendering large blocks of territory in return for peace.

That treaty was a double gain for Germany. For not only did it grant her valuable lands in the east, it freed hundreds of thousands of veteran soldiers for the Western Front.

How should these soldiers be used? Ludendorff and the High Command weren't sure. There were two choices, both very promising and very dangerous. They might, first, play it safe. Safety meant digging into such strong positions that the Allies would lose hope of victory and come to the conference table. Although Germany would have to return most occupied territory to France and Belgium, she'd still keep certain key areas, such as Alsace-Lorraine, with its rich coal and iron fields.

The only problem with this idea was that the Allies might also decide to dig in, tying down Germany's armies while the Allied blockade of shipping did its work slowly. The blockade was steadily growing more effective. Reports of hunger flooded into Berlin from every part of the country. In the capital itself, the weekly meat ration was down to a quarter-pound of poor-quality hamburger. Military supplies, too, were fewer and of poorer quality. Bandages, for example, were no longer of soft cotton gauze, but of white tissue paper.

The other choice was to launch an all-out offensive to win the war before the Americans tipped the balance. This, too, was dangerous. When a general asked Ludendorff what would happen if the offensive failed, he fixed him with his cold stare and snapped, "Then Germany must perish!"

The decision was to throw the iron dice. Germany would gamble everything on a quick victory. Win or lose, the war would be over by the close of 1918.

Ludendorff kept his preparations under a tight lid of secrecy.

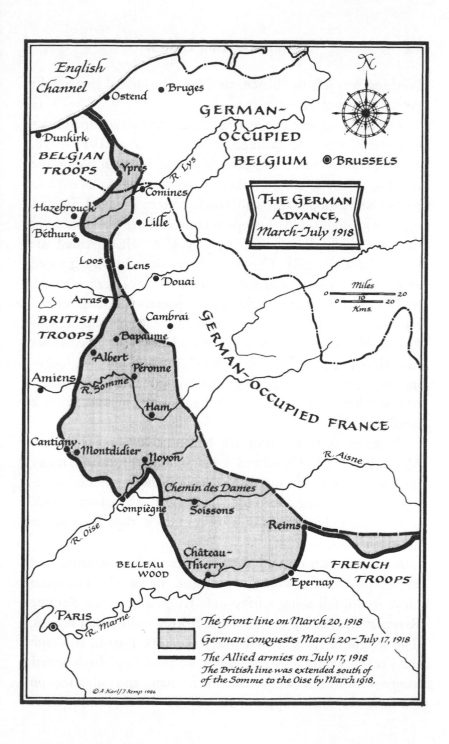

Nothing was left to chance, nothing overlooked that might give warning of his intentions.

The build-up, one of the largest and most secret operations in history, went on throughout the winter of 1917–1918. Roads, railway lines, and airfields were built all along the front so as not to arouse Allied suspicions about one area in particular. Troop trains and truck convoys moved only at night with lights out. Troops marched along back roads in darkness, hiding in forests in daylight, when Allied air patrols became active. Cannon wheels were heavily greased and horses's hooves wrapped in canvas sacks against noise; harness buckles were blackened to prevent glinting in the moonlight. Artillery positions were dug at night and camouflaged. Mounds of shells were stored near the guns under camouflage nets. Officers flew over the positions each morning to report any telltale sign that might alert the enemy. Every wheel mark had to be raked away or covered with brush.

Preparations were complete before dawn on Thursday, March 21, 1918. Three and a half million Germans, many trained as Storm Troopers, crouched in their trenches, waiting. A ground fog shrouded much of the Western Front; it promised to hide the assault waves during their dash across no-man's-land.

A million men of the German Second, Seventeenth, and Eighteenth Armies were to spearhead the assault. The main blow would fall along a fifty-mile front west of the Somme River, at the joining point of the British and French armies. The weight of the attack would fall on the British, although the French would also take a terrific pounding. Ludendorff meant to force a wedge between them and advance on Amiens, the main supply base of the British army. Once

Storm Troopers, crouching low, wait for the order to attack during Ludendorff's last offensive.

Amiens fell, it would be easy to push the British northward, into the English Channel, while other forces drove south to Paris.

Men stared tensely as the luminous dials of their wrist-watches ticked off the minutes. Shells slid into the firing chambers of cannon with a soft *swish*. Silently, long gun muzzles rose, moved from side to side, and steadied. Artillerymen stuffed wads of cotton into their ears.

It began.

At exactly 4:40 A.M. Ludendorff unleashed the heaviest bombardment in the history of the world. Six thousand cannon opened fire at once along the Somme and kept firing for five hours without letup. The British replied with twenty-five hundred guns of their own.

Nothing could check the fury of the German bombardment. The ground shook as in an earthquake; miles behind the battle zone men felt the vibrations in the soles of their feet.

The effect was terrible. Shells, hundreds of them at a time, landed in straight rows five yards apart, the edges of their craters touching to form series of neat figure eights. The British guns became heaps of blood-spattered junk. Command posts vanished into smoking shell holes. Trenches caved in on their inhabitants, becoming mass graves. Ammunition dumps roared and crackled like strings of firecrackers. Barbed wire entanglements were shredded.

Tommies, British footsoldiers, huddled dazed in their trenches or stumbled about like sleepwalkers with ears ringing. Choking with fear, they donned gas masks and felt their lungs fill with clean air as the world outside turned poisonous. Amid the shelling they heard piercing shrieks and a muffled patter: millions of rats came swarming out of no-man's-land.

The vile creatures bounded into the trenches, leaped up the rear walls, and continued to the rear. Only the men remained.

At 10:00 A.M. whistles blew and waves of Storm Troopers rose from their trenches. Some toppled over instantly, but most ran forward as flamethrowers led the way. Within minutes they crossed no-man's-land and jumped into the British trenches, shouting, shooting, and bombing with "potato mashers," a grenade shaped like a tin can at the end of a long wooden handle.

The Storm Troopers slashed through the Somme defenses. Behind them came regular infantry to mop up and destroy any strong points that might have been bypassed. For the first time since the war began, an advance was measured not in yards, but miles. Within three days the Germans jabbed a salient, or wedge, forty miles into the Allied front.

But the British held on to Amiens with bulldog determination. Their commander, Field Marshal Sir Douglas Haig, threw every man who could carry a rifle into the fight. Cooks, office clerks, and wagon drivers suddenly found themselves eating dust at the front. Hospitals were combed for the walking wounded, injured soldiers who could still shoot straight. They saved Amiens, halting the enemy within sight of its church steeples. Yet the cost was high: 240,000 Englishmen and nearly as many Germans.

Paris, however, soon felt the enemy's hot breath. On March 23, an explosion rocked the city, followed by others at twenty-minute intervals. At first Parisians thought enemy bombers had broken through the city's air defenses. But the truth, when it became known a few days later, was a lot worse.

The Germans had done the impossible; built a super gun as long as a ten-story building is tall to fire shells eighty miles, triple the range of the largest battleship cannon. Nicknamed "Big Bertha," this monster was hidden in a forest, firing when the sky was clear of Allied planes.

Big Bertha continued dropping shells onto Paris until August, when Allied counterattacks forced her to be moved out of range. Even so, she caused a near-panic in the city, killing and wounding nearly a thousand civilians. The worst tragedy happened when a shell struck a church, sending the heavy roof crashing onto worshippers below.

Ludendorff sent the British reeling with another mass attack in early April along the Lys River in Belgium. Field Marshal Haig, his front crumbling, issued his Order of the Day, one of the most famous messages of the war. The British, he said, had no choice but to fight it out. "Every position must be held to the last man. There must be no retirement. With our backs to the wall and believing in the justice of our cause, each one of us must fight to the end."

The battered Tommies might have been driven into the sea had the French not rushed to their aid. General Ferdinand Foch, recently appointed supreme commander of Allied forces on the Western Front, sent his last reserves, the Army of the North, to support the British. About five hundred Doughboys in training with the British also helped.

Once again Ludendorff's attack slowed down, then ground to a halt. This time each side lost about one hundred thousand men.

The Allies didn't dare relax their efforts. Ludendorff, they knew, had bet too much on this campaign to give up easily. This time they'd beat him to the punch. Before he struck again, the Allies would try to throw him off balance by counterattacking. And since the French reserves were busy

Field Marshal Ferdinand Foch was supreme commander of Allied armies on the Western Front.

up north, the Americans would have to take on the assignment.

General Pershing had wanted to get into the fight from the beginning. When the Germans crossed the Somme, he drove to Foch's headquarters to offer help. It was a dramatic meeting, with Black Jack practically begging the Frenchman to allow the AEF to fight. "I come to say to you that the American people would hold it a great honor for our troops were they engaged in the present battle. I ask it of you in my name and in that of the American people. There is at this moment no other question than that of fighting. Infantry, artillery, aviation—all that we have are yours to dispose of as you will. Others are coming which are as numerous as will be necessary. I have come to say to you that the American people would be proud to be engaged in the greatest battle in history." Foch was overcome with emotion and kissed the American on both cheeks.

The only problem was that the commanders disagreed on how to use the Doughboys. Foch and Haig wanted them only as replacements to plug gaps in their own ranks. The Americans would be scattered among French and British units, serve under foreign officers, and take orders from a high command controlled by foreigners.

Black Jack objected; indeed, he pounded the table with his fists and shouted phrases he'd learned as a young cavalryman in Apache country. The Doughboys had come over to fight for freedom, not to become food for the guns. They'd fight as Americans, in an American army, under American officers.

Only four infantry regiments—the 369th, 370th, 371st, 372nd—were ever put under foreign control. These were the black poilus, all-Negro combat units, which became part of the French army. Racial segregation was at its height in the United States at this time. Although blacks were drafted, they weren't allowed to serve with white soldiers; but their officers were white. Blacks were barred altogether from the Marine Corps and served in the Navy only as cooks and laborers.

General Pershing sent black outfits to the French, because many congressmen didn't want them fighting alongside whites as equals. To Foch, anyone was welcome who'd fight for France. The French army already had units from the colonies in Vietnam, Morocco and Senegal, West Africa. American

Black Jack Pershing as a four-star general, 1918. Pershing had many heated arguments with Allied generals, who wanted to break up the AEF to use it as a pool of replacements for their battered armies.

Blacks turned out to be equally fine troops, brave and steady under fire. Several won the Croix de Guerre (War Cross), France's highest award for gallantry.

Black Jack finally had his way for the counterattack. He'd hit the Germans square in the nose at Cantigny, the tip of the salient below Amiens. Cantigny would be the first full-scale battle of the AEF.

Toward the end of May 1918, the Big Red One, the division nearest the battle area, received orders to get rolling.

Those orders were like an electrical charge starting a giant engine. Troops hurriedly packed their gear. Last-minute letters were scribbled in pencil after boarding trucks. Sad goodbyes were said.

At dawn on May 28, American artillerymen plastered Cantigny with high explosives and mustard gas. As the sun peeked above the horizon, First Division infantrymen began their walk across the fields. They walked silently, dry-mouthed, with hearts pounding. A detachment of French tanks clattered nearby for support, while French long-range guns added their voices to the battle.

The Germans fought from house to house, cellar to cellar. The Doughboys blasted them out with grenades, dug them out with bayonets, until none remained in Cantigny.

Yet there was no time to pat themselves on the back. The Huns weren't good losers and would surely return. The Yanks hastily dug trenches, strung barbed wire, and waited. They didn't have to wait long.

Enemy guns sent down a storm of shells, flattening the ruins of Cantigny and covering them with a pall of dust. The Yanks held on.

Enemy infantry advanced. The Yanks shot them down at the wire. Snipers' well-placed shots turned flamethrowermen into human torches.

Cantigny stayed American. "We're in at last!" shouted newspaper headlines at home.

In the meantime, Ludendorff hurled another thunderbolt. After the disasters of 1917, the Chemin des Dames had become a quiet sector thinly held by weary French and British troops. Yet that peacefulness was a trick, part of a plan to make them lower their guard. The Germans had used the

months of quiet to reinforce their First and Seventh Armies
with fresh troops and masses of heavy guns. Even the frogs
cooperated with the build-up. Their croaking was so loud
that German engineers set up portable bridges along a stream
separating the armies without being overheard.

Only the Americans suspected trouble. Pershing's intelligence officers had studied hundreds of reports of enemy
activity and decided that Ludendorff would try a breakout
in the Chemin des Dames. The French and British pooh-
poohed the warning. The Yanks were newcomers to military
intelligence, they said. Their own staffs knew better.

The Germans attacked at dawn, May 27, 1918. It was the
Somme all over again, only far, far worse. The Allies, taken
by surprise, broke and fell back in confusion. The enemy
swept forward, unstoppable. German divisions moved so fast
that the retreating Allies had no time to dynamite the bridges
at key river crossings. Within four days Ludendorff's legions
crossed three rivers—the Aisne, Vesle, and Ourcq—and
gobbled up the railway center of Soissons, capturing squadrons of brand-new fighter planes and mountains of supplies.
On the fifth day their spearheads reached the Marne River.
For the first time since 1914, the enemy came within striking
distance of Paris, forty miles to the southwest. Had they had
tanks, as they would in 1940, nothing could have stopped
them.

Panic gripped the French capital. As the breeze brought
echoes of distant gunfire, a million people streamed along the
highways to the south, seeking safety anywhere. The government prepared to flee to Bordeaux; already secret papers were
being destroyed to keep them out of enemy hands. General
Jean Degoutte, commanding on the Chemin des Dames front,
had given up hope. Nothing he did seemed able to halt the

collapse. He sat in his command post, shells exploding nearby, silently weeping over a crumpled map.

Now came Foch's turn to gamble. Nearly all French reserves were supporting the British in the north. To move them south would weaken the British, inviting Ludendorff to renew his attack. Yet Paris had to be saved. Somehow he had to find the troops to bar the way.

The Yanks had done well at Cantigny. That was a ray of hope. But how would they do against the flower of the German army, men who could already taste victory? He'd have to take the chance. Ready or not, he'd throw the AEF into the path of Ludendorff's steamroller.

Truck convoys of the American Third Division snaked along the highways toward the sound of the guns. Their destination was Château-Thierry, a town built on both banks of the Marne and joined by two fine bridges. Once the enemy crossed these bridges, he'd have clear sailing right up to the gates of Paris. The Third Division must hold these crossings —or die trying.

The Seventh Machine Gun Battalion reached the battlefield hours ahead of the rest of the division; its trucks had fewer breakdowns and blowouts than the others. It arrived on the morning of May 31, just in time to dig in and sight its forty-eight machine guns on the bridges and the streets leading to them on the opposite bank. Within an hour French troops filled those streets, running as if the Devil himself was after them. No sooner did they cross the bridges, blowing up one as they went, than the Germans appeared.

Hour after hour they tried to storm the remaining bridge, a large, solid structure of steel and stone. And each time they advanced, they ran into a wall of hot lead. Machine gun slugs ricocheted off steel girders. Bullets stitched the ground, tossing up little geysers of dust.

It was a slaughter. Gray-clad bodies choked the streets leading to the bridge. Corpses were piled on the bridge itself, forcing the living to climb over them until they, too, were mowed down.

German artillery replied with a devastating barrage. The Yanks crouched low, peered over their gunsights, and kept shooting.

Over a thousand Germans fell that day. They would have kept coming had some brave Frenchmen not dynamited the bridge. Tons of steel and stone shot skyward, a joyous sight to the grimy machine gunners.

Members of the Seventh Machine Gun Battalion covering the approaches to one of the bridges at Château-Thierry, June 1, 1918. Their only camouflage is a piece of cloth with a small hole through which to fire their weapon, a French chauchat.

They'd won. They'd turned the tide at Château-Thierry. Although they couldn't know it then, the enemy would never come any closer to Paris than these broken bridges.

The most famous American battle of the First World War took place eight miles northwest of Château-Thierry. The battleground was an abandoned hunting preserve, about a squaremile in area, on a gently rolling hill that commands the surrounding countryside. It is called the Bois de Belleau. Belleau Wood.

During that flaming spring of 1918, this lovely spot was a dagger pointed at the Allies' lifeline. A natural observation post, Belleau Wood could also be used as a staging area for attacks on the Paris-Metz highway, a major link between the capital and the front. The Germans held it. And the Yanks had to take it away from them.

This difficult assignment was given to the Second Infantry Division, under General Omar Bundy. The Second Division, with its Indian head shoulder patch, consisted of two brigades. A brigade is made up of two four-thousand-man regiments, each commanded by a colonel. This division's first brigade was formed of Regular Army soldiers, professionals with several years of service. The second brigade was more comfortable on the heaving deck of a ship than in a muddy trench. They were soldiers of the sea, the Fifth and Sixth Regiments of the United States Marine Corps. Black Jack considered them the best fighting men in the AEF. They, the Leathernecks, must clear the Germans out of Belleau Wood.

Pershing's confidence was well-placed, for the Marines were indeed special. Theirs was a proud heritage going back to the Corps' founding in 1775, which made it older than the Declaration of Independence. All volunteers, the Marines of 1918 upheld that heritage even at the cost of their lives.

There is a story about a kindly American lady who often visited French military hospitals to help with the wounded. Upon entering a casualty ward one day, she noticed a strange face. Unlike a Frenchman, who considered himself naked without a mustache, this soldier was clean-shaven.

"Oh," she cried, happy to see a fellow countryman, "surely you are an American."

"No ma'am," he answered. "I'm a Marine." The Corps. It was his home, and war was his profession.

Marine training was as good as any Blue Devil's or Storm Trooper's. When a youngster joined the Corps, he was sent to Parris Island off the coast of Port Royal, South Carolina. Upon arrival, the trainee, or "boot," had his head shaved and was assigned to a "DI," drill instructor, a sergeant or corporal picked for his experience and meanness. From then on life became a daily battle with man and nature.

Parris Island was—and is—a sunbaked, windblown, sandy strip of land owned by the fiercest flies in creation. The DIs, wiry men with bone-deep suntans, drilled the boots day and night, tightening muscles and working off fat.

One idea was drilled into his head until it became second nature. The rifle. The 1903-model Springfield rifle was *the* Marine's weapon. A Marine must master the "03," making it an extension of himself. He must learn how to shoot straight, shoot often, and shoot to kill.

Boot camp took a lot out of a man, but it also gave him a lot: pride, self-confidence, strength, determination. As a recruit wrote in a letter to his mother: "The first day I was in camp I was afraid I was going to die. The next two weeks my sole fear was that I wasn't going to die. After that I knew I'd never die because I'd become so hard that nothing could kill me."

On May 31, 1918, the Fifth and Sixth Marines piled into

trucks for a ride along the Paris-Metz highway. That trip was a sobering experience in several ways. It was a scorching hot day, and the sun beat down on the men crowding the hard benches of the open trucks. The road had turned to a bed of powdery gray dust, which rose in clouds as the trucks lumbered along, covering the men. They were miserable, coughing and wheezing; beads of sweat carved muddy channels down their cheeks.

Most of these Marines, who'd never been in battle, now saw the human tragedy of war for the first time. The highway was crowded with refugees, French people fleeing the advancing Germans. Men and women, young and old, trudged along the roadside, into the dust storms raised by the speeding trucks. Some walked in wooden shoes, holding a child by the hand, a few possessions balanced on their heads or slung over their backs. Others drove farm wagons or pulled wheelbarrows piled with featherbeds and chairs and grandfather clocks and rabbits in cages and chickens tied by the legs. The sick and elderly, their strength gone, lay panting in ditches or under trees. All had terror in their eyes.

The column arrived next morning, July 1, at the tiny village of Lucy-Le-Bocage southeast of Belleau Wood. The local French commander greeted them and suggested that they dig a trench line. The Leatherneck officers brushed aside the suggestion. Trenches were for defending, and they meant to attack. The most they'd do was dig shallow one- and two-man rifle pits, which someone called "foxholes." The name caught on and has been used ever since.

Having settled into their foxholes, the Marines' thoughts turned to food. They'd been eating cold monkey meat for the past few days and wanted a change. Search parties went out to scour the countryside. They returned with cows, rabbits, and chickens. The whole area had been abandoned by the farmers, along with most of their livestock, which wandered about free for the taking. The Marines ate to their hearts' content.

Yet there were constant reminders that they were camped on the edge of a volcano. There was no letup to the distant shellfire and crackle of small arms. Occasionally the wind brought a smell that made them lose their appetites. "Phew! dead hawses," a private said, crinkling his nose. "Those are not dead horses," his lieutenant replied.

The war came to them on June 3. That morning the shellfire grew louder and retreating French soldiers began to filter through their positions. They were a sorry-looking lot. Dirty and unshaven, their uniforms in rags, they had no weapons, having thrown them away in order to travel lightly. Many were drunk—drunk from fatigue and from wine looted from abandoned farmhouses.

French refugees such as the Marines saw from their trucks on the way to Belleau Wood.

Officers and common soldiers alike had lost hope. *"La guerre est fini!" "Fini est la guerre!"* they called to the Leathernecks in their foxholes. "The war is over!" "Over is the war!"

When a panicky French major ordered him to join the retreat, Captain Lloyd Williams snapped: "Retreat, hell. We just got here." The words spread like wildfire from unit to unit. When the Leathernecks in the foxholes heard it, they nodded, patting their Springfields affectionately.

The Germans attacked that afternoon. For the next two days they threw "sea-bags," large-caliber shells, and whiz-bangs at the Marines. Lucy-Le-Bocage became a heap of smoking rubble.

Bombardments were always followed by infantry assaults. Each time the Leathernecks held their fire until the enemy came to within three hundred yards, an unheard-of distance for rifle fire on the Western Front. At last the hours on the Parris Island rifle range paid off. The German veterans knew everything there was to know about machine guns and artillery. They knew their sound, their range, and how to take cover from them. But they were puzzled by accurate, long-range rifle fire that came from nowhere, dropping men right and left. The war had suddenly become very personal. Each of these Springfield bullets seemed to have a man's name on it. The German infantry lost their nerve and ran for cover, leaving their dead behind.

The Marines' assignment, however, hadn't changed: capture Belleau Wood. The plan, worked out by General James G. Harboard, the brigade commander, had three parts. The battle would begin with an assault on Hill 142, a post for German artillery spotters to the left of the wood. This would be followed by the main effort against the wood itself.

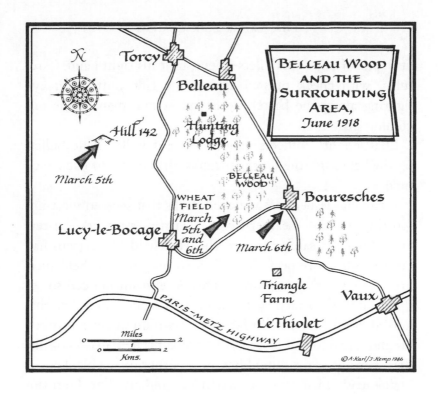

Finally, the Marines would capture Bouresches, a village at a road junction to the right of the wood.

At 5:00 A.M., June 6, 1918, the Leathernecks rose from their foxholes and started for Hill 142. Enemy machine gun bullets were already whipping overhead when the sun began to rise, red and round, over the eastern horizon. Men went down, some lying still, others thrashing in pain. Their comrades, taking advantage of the half-darkness, ran forward. Time dragged, minutes feeling like hours, until they took the enemy positions at the point of the bayonet.

But the German, Jerry, had only just begun to fight. He wanted that hill back and came after it, determined to have his way. He didn't.

The Marines sprawled flat-out on the ground, each with a

little pile of clips, six bullets apiece, near his right hand. Carefully, with cheek pressed against the rifle butt, right eye sighting along the barrel, he aimed at one man in the oncoming gray mob.

"Battlesight!" officers yelled. "Fire at will!" Rifle bullets scythed through the German ranks, driving them back each time.

Growing desperate, they used tricks that seemed most unsporting to the Leathernecks. German stretcher bearers moved openly, safely, around the battlefield; Americans had been taught to respect the red cross insignia and held their fire whenever they appeared. Then a sergeant noticed something odd. Two men were carrying a loaded stretcher that looked like a person with his legs drawn up under a blanket. He motioned to an officer, who turned his field glasses on the stretcher just as the wind blew up a corner of the blanket.

Baloney! That was no wounded soldier. The Germans were hiding behind the red cross insignia in order to bring forward heavy machine guns. As sensible people, the Leathernecks were willing to learn from the enemy. From then on stretcher bearers carrying covered objects were riddled with bullets.

The Germans began to realize that the Marines were not to be trifled with. Later a letter was found on the body of a German private. "The Americans are savages," it said. "They kill everything that moves."

The attacks gradually tapered off, leaving the Leathernecks in possession of the hill. They also gained a new name. From then on, the Germans called them *Teufelhünden*—Devil Dogs, or Hounds of Hell.

The main event began at 5:00 P.M. Everything until now had been easy, compared to Belleau Wood itself. It was to be the supreme test of the Marines' training, skill, and courage.

Every man knew he'd be walking into a hornets' nest, for the wood was a natural fortress. Take a million giant boulders and scatter them helter-skelter over uneven ground. Cover them with moss, wet and slippery, and fill the spaces between with tall, slender trees so close together that visibility is cut to less than twenty feet. Hide in this tangle veterans manning scores of machine guns arranged in supporting fields of fire. (Anyone who attacked one machine gun would immediately come under fire from at least two others.) That was Belleau Wood.

The Fifth and Sixth Marines awaited the attack signal in an arc running around the wood's southern edge. Between them and the trees lay wheatfields from an eighth- to a quarter-mile wide. It was a beautiful spring day, warm and bright. The wheat lay thigh-deep, green, rustling, and dotted with scarlet poppies. The Leathernecks would have to cross these wheatfields in the open before they could find, let alone fight, the enemy. In the meantime they sat in small groups, talking softly and eyeing the quiet wood.

Whistles blew.

The Marines arranged themselves in four ranks, twenty yards between each rank, and began their long walk. Nothing stirred, save the wheat as it gently brushed their legs. The only sound was the chirping of grasshoppers mingled with the far-away rumble of artillery. And the sound of their own quick, nervous breathing.

On they came in perfectly aligned ranks, rifles at the ready position: held diagonally across the chest, bayonet over the left shoulder, right index finger gripping the trigger. A corporal bent over to pick a poppy to stick in his helmet strap. An officer calmly puffed his pipe, waving his men forward with his swagger stick.

Hell broke loose.

The Marines had gone a hundred yards when a *crack* sounding like thousands of snapping twigs came from the woods. Invisible machine gunners cut loose, filling the air with whining slugs; one American described them as "red-hot nails."

Machine gun bullets shredded the young wheat. Their force spun men around, sending them toppling to the ground. Yet close as they hugged the earth, they couldn't get close enough for safety. Gas masks, which were worn at the ready on the chest, raised head and shoulders three inches. Those three inches were often the difference between life and death. Marines felt bullets slicing through their backpacks. Others never felt a thing.

The world would soon learn of Sergeant Dan Daly, a Medal of Honor winner who'd been bossing around recruits for twenty-five years. Daly's men were pinned down when he stood up and, waving his rifle above his head, shouted, "Come on you Leathernecks! Do you want to live forever?" No, they didn't want to live forever, only long enough to get into those woods for a crack at the Germans. Forgetting their fear, they rose and, hunching their shoulders as if the bullets were wind-driven snowflakes, went forward.

Nearby, Floyd Gibbons of the Chicago *Tribune* advanced with another unit, armed only with pad and pencil. Gibbons, a famous newspaperman, was taking in the scene when machine guns caught his line in a crossfire. As he dived for cover, he saw an officer standing holding a bloody stump and screaming, "My hand's gone."

"Get down. Flatten out, Major!" Gibbons shouted. "I'm crawling over to you now."

Slowly the reporter pushed forward by digging in with his elbows and toes. He'd gone just a few yards when a bullet went through his left arm, followed seconds later by another through the left shoulder. He was surprised at how little it hurt; pain would come later, when the shock wore off.

But that's when the big one found him. Gibbons heard a loud crash, like a glass bottle shattering in a bathtub. Everything turned white. Gibbons tried to move the fingers of his left hand. They moved; so did his left foot. Yes, he was alive.

Then he touched his nose. His fingers rested on something soft and wet. His hand was covered with blood. A facial wound!

The left side of his face hurt, so he closed his right eye. Darkness. A bullet had ricocheted off a stone, entered his left eye and passed through his head, making a hole in his helmet as it went. Moments later he saw the handless major run into the forest.

Gibbons lay in the wheat, bullets passing inches from his head, until stretcher bearers collected the wounded after dark. He later wrote *And They Thought We Wouldn't Fight*, one of the best firsthand accounts of the First World War.

Other Marines, meanwhile, reached the wood in small groups. They didn't get very far. As night fell, their rifle flashes gave away their positions, attracting storms of machine gun bullets. Hungry, their ammunition nearly gone, they retreated across the blood-soaked wheatfield under cover of darkness.

Their buddies on the right, however, captured Bouresches after savage hand-to-hand fighting. As the last Germans fled, their artillery thundered, churning up the ruins of the town. With food and ammunition low, the Marines began to worry.

Just when things seemed darkest, "Elizabeth 'Lizzie' Ford"

delivered the goods. Lizzie was an old rattletrap of a Ford truck, a candidate for the junkheap. But today she was gorgeous, a heroine, in the Leathernecks' eyes. Peering from the ruins of Bouresches, they saw Private Morris Fleitz driving her pell-mell across the wheatfields with a load of supplies. Shrapnel shells burst overhead, covering her with steel splinters. Exploding whizbangs rocked her from side to side. The Marines punched the air, cheering as she barreled through the dust and smoke. Later, when the firing slackened, they painted a Croix de Guerre on her hood.

June 6, 1918, was the worst day in Marine Corps history. With 1,087 killed and wounded, it had lost more men than in the past 143 years put together. There wouldn't be such a day again until November 20, 1943, when Leathernecks stormed the Japanese fortress island of Tawara.

Tough as he was, General Pershing, who knew what it meant to lose a child, was deeply moved by the casualty report. When he heard of their losses, his voice broke and his eyes filled. Those Leathernecks were like Black Jack's own sons.

Yet the struggle for Belleau Wood was only beginning. During the following weeks, Second Division gunners drenched it with explosives and gas. Each time the shelling stopped, the Marines charged into the underbrush. Once they gained a foothold, they hung on, advancing a little further each day.

Belleau Wood became a bushwhackers' war, the same kind of struggle Indians and frontiersmen had known, only with more powerful weapons. Small squads stalked each other like animals, springing from ambush to kill and run away. In addition to rifles and grenades, Marines used bowie knives and sawed-off shotguns for close combat. Cries of *eyah, eyah*

Marine sentries remained at their posts during poison gas attacks, and at attention.

rang through the wood. It was part of the Marine bayonet drill, learned at Parris Island.

Danger was sometimes mixed with humor. One morning a Marine platoon was awakened by shouts in English followed by bursts of machine gun fire. A trigger-happy patrol had started shooting without making sure of its target. The platoon members were preparing to return fire when an officer recognized the voice of one of the attackers. They were from the same battalion.

"Jackson!" he shouted.

"Yes, Captain," came the reply.

"Where are you?"

"Right here. Across the road."

"Stand up, so I can see you."

"Captain," Jackson cried above the chattering machine guns, "if you want to see me, *you* stand up."

Chuckles were heard along both sides of the road. Men backed off, thankful that nobody had been hurt—this time.

The Germans recognized that they'd met their match in the Devil Dogs. We know how they felt from letters and reports captured during the battle. In a letter home, which he didn't live to mail, a private complained: "We are having very heavy days with death before us hourly. Here we have no hope ever to come out. My company has been reduced from 120 to 30 men. . . . We have Americans (Marines) opposite us who are terribly reckless fellows. In the last eight days I have not slept 20 hours." A comrade, also killed, wrote of the Marines that "they fight like devils."

The best compliment came from a secret intelligence report based on questioning captured Marines. The report's author, a hardboiled professional soldier named von Berg, compared the Leathernecks to the best units in the kaiser's army:

The Second American Division must be considered a very good one and may even perhaps be reckoned a Storm Troop. The different attacks at Belleau Wood were carried out with bravery and dash. The moral effect of our gunfire cannot seriously impede the advance of the American infantry. The Americans' nerves are not yet worn out.

The qualities of the men individually may be described as remarkable. They are physically well-developed, their attitude is good, and they range in age from eighteen to twenty-eight years. . . . The men are in fine spirits and are full of self-confidence. The words of a prisoner are characteristic—WE KILL OR GET KILLED.

The end came in Belleau Wood on June 26, after a bombardment lasting fourteen hours. The Germans, forced into a corner near the northern edge, were groggy with fatigue; many were shell shocked. Burned trees, their branches gone, stood like skeletons guarding the ruins. The odor of mustard gas clung to the shattered tree trunks. Gas collected in shell holes, remaining there, still deadly, long after the air cleared; many an unwary soldier died when jumping into these holes without his gas mask.

As the bombardment lifted, the Marines moved out for the final sweep. At 7:00 A.M. Major Maurice Shearer sent a message to General Harboard. Short and sharp, like a whizbang, it said everything: "Belleau Woods now U.S. Marine Corps entirely." Five days later the Second Division's Army

Vaux, after the battle. Stretcher bearers removing a wounded Doughboy from the ruined town.

"We have lost quite a few officers," said a report from Belleau Wood. Here three Marine officers visit the graves of fallen comrades, whose names are visible on the wooden markers.

brigade took the fortified town of Vaux southeast of Boureshes, on the Paris-Metz highway. The operation went off so smoothly that fewer than fifty Doughboys lost their lives.

But the Leathernecks were the heroes of the hour, although, as yet, they didn't feel very heroic. With the woods secure, they packed up for a rest camp behind the lines. Fewer trucks were needed to take them away, and these weren't as crowded as before. Belleau Wood had cost the Marine brigade fifty-two hundred killed and wounded, among them half its officers. All the survivors wanted was a hot meal, sleep, and a bath. They were too busy tending to their own needs to realize what they'd accomplished.

The French people let them know when they came to Paris on leave. Another July Fourth had arrived, and once again the City of Light turned out for a parade. It was really the Marines' parade, for they stole the show. Marine Captain Clifford Cates described it in a letter to his mother:

> The morning of the 4th, we got up early and cleaned up and tried to look half way decent, but we still looked like a bunch of bums. At eight we left our camp and marched to where the parade formed. Mother, you cannot imagine the cheer that would go up as the French people would recognize the Marine flag—it was one continuous shout—Vive les Marines—la Marines, etc. They literally covered us with roses—I would carry each bouquet a piece and then drop it—then another girl would load me down with more flowers. It was truly wonderful and it made us Marines feel very good as they gave us all the credit. Even every little kid going to and from Paris would yell, "Vive la Marines." We have certainly made a name in France.

As a sign of their appreciation, the French changed the name of the Bois de Belleau to Bois de la Brigade de Marine.

Ludendorff's plans lay in ruins. He'd gambled his country's future on a knockout blow and lost. The Allies took the blow, held, and came back fighting. And it was Black Jack's Yanks who'd played a key role in turning the tide.

Europe had learned a lot about the Yanks in a year, and they'd learned a lot about themselves. On Independence Day 1917, the Allies saw hope in the brawny youngsters from the New World. But what could they do? Would they fight, and how well?

Everyone knew the answers by Independence Day 1918. Cantigny, Château-Thierry, and Belleau Wood showed that they could fight and win. At last Pershing was allowed to form and command an independent force, the United States First Army. The Yanks were now equal partners in the First World War.

FIVE

The Home Front

★ The First World War was fought on other fronts and by other warriors than those who faced each other across no-man's-land. These fronts were not raked by gunfire or smothered in poison gas. Warriors there fought, not with deadly weapons, but with the tools of peace. These were the civilian-soldiers—men, women, children—who fought on the home fronts.

"Home front" is a term invented in Europe to describe a new reality, the reality of total war. When nations fought in earlier centuries, most civilians were untouched by war's horrors unless they lived in a battle zone. Usually they paid their taxes and went about their business as if the fighting were in a far-away galaxy.

That began to change in 1914. Mass armies and mass production created total war. In a total war every available person and resource is mobilized for the national effort; even children have a part to play. Thus the home front became as important as the battle front. Its victories and defeats were as vital to the war's outcome as battles won and lost. Civilian-soldiers worked in factories and on the land, producing whatever the armed forces needed. Without support from the home front, the battle front would have collapsed overnight.

Supplying the war effort was a tangle of complicated problems. The largest problem involved using the nation's resources in the best way possible. On the one hand, resources were limited. The United States, although the world's richest nation, couldn't produce enough to meet all its needs at once. On the other hand, the war's demands were unlimited. Not a day passed without the cry of *more*—more ships, more ammunition, more food, more everything.

Meeting one set of needs meant shortchanging others that might be just as important. Take, for example, nitrates, chemicals used in explosives as well as fertilizers. Should the limited nitrate supplies go into ammunition, without which guns are useless, or to grow food, without which gunners are useless? Should we send locomotives to the AEF to haul shells to the front, or to Chile to haul nitrates without which there'd be no shells?

Similar questions were asked about metals, machinery, ships, and cloth. Should steel go to build destroyers to sink submarines or to build merchantmen, which the U-boats were trying to destroy? Should cranes be used to load ships at American docks or unload them at French docks? Should cotton go into tires for army trucks or into fabric for army airplanes? Fighters or bombers? Which, and how many? There were lots of hard questions and no easy answers.

Until 1918 the United States was a jigsaw puzzle of separate industries, markets, transportation networks, and sources of raw materials. Each businessman made his own decisions, in his own way, and for his own benefit.

War forced Americans to look at their country differently. Instead of many businesses competing with each other, the United States had to be one factory operating under one management. Instead of manufacturing many separate products, everything it produced must be part of a single gigantic machine: the war effort. The United States of America must become Factory America.

The chief manager of Factory America was a tall, rosy-cheeked millionaire named Bernard Baruch. Born in 1870, Baruch began his career as a three-dollar-a-week errand boy for a Wall Street stockbroker in New York City. A go-getter with a razor-sharp mind and a photographic memory, Baruch made the first of his many millions before the age of thirty.

Baruch knew just about everything a person could know about American business. He also knew everyone he needed to know: industrialists, lumbermen, bankers, railway tycoons, mine owners. President Wilson, who called Baruch "Doctor Facts," put him in charge of the War Industries Board.

Next to the President himself, Baruch became the most powerful man in the country. Within days of taking office, he sent telegrams to top businessmen asking them to come to Washington. He gave them an offer few could refuse. The country, he explained, was in a life-and-death struggle for the freedom of the world. They were experts in their fields. The work would be hard, the hours long, and they'd have to be away from their own businesses for a long time. But America needed their talents for the war effort. Would they help?

Would they! Nearly all agreed to serve as long as necessary. Their salary: the grand sum of a dollar a year. America had been good to them, and now they repaid the favor. No-

As head of the War Industries Board, Bernard Baruch (lower right) became one of the most powerful men in First World War America.

body cashed his paycheck. These were framed and displayed as proudly as any Doughboy's medals.

The War Industries Board took charge of the nation's economy for the remainder of the war. Doctor Facts and his team of Dollar-a-Year Men ran things like dictators. Their authority extended from coast to coast, from steel rails to lead pencils. They took an inventory of the nation's resources and decided how to distribute them in the most sensible way. Businessmen were forbidden to use materials and labor for products not absolutely necessary for civilian well-being or the war effort. Disobedience meant stiff fines and a cutoff of raw materials.

It was discovered, for example, that eight thousand tons

of steel were used each year in making corsets so that ladies might look slim. Baruch stopped corset-making and set the factories to producing stretchers for the army medical corps. Whenever possible, manufacturers were shown how to convert their plants to military use. Women's dress factories switched over to uniforms, sewing machine plants turned out machine guns, piano factories built airplane wings.

Civilians were limited in their use of raw materials. Wood replaced iron in baby carriages. Brass and copper coffins were discontinued. Bicycles, clocks, furniture, and other products were streamlined and simplified to save raw materials. Congress helped by passing a Daylight Savings Time law; the nation's clocks were moved ahead in spring to give an extra hour of daylight, thus saving coal and electricity.

The transportation industry received special attention. The railroads, which carried most of the nation's passengers and freight, were taken over by the government for as long as the war lasted. Railroad owners were, of course, paid for the use of their property, but the government decided what the trains should carry, when, and where.

Ships, too, were important in the war effort. When we entered the war, the Allies were promised a "Bridge of Ships" to France. To keep that promise, the government did things no one would have thought possible a few months before. All shipyards were taken over and assigned war work. Every vessel over twenty-five hundred tons was "drafted" into government service at a price set by Washington. Great Lakes steamers were brought to the Atlantic coast; twelve of the largest vessels were cut in half to fit through canal locks and reassembled upon reaching their destination.

Uncle Sam himself went into the shipbuilding business. The government took over Hog Island, a swampy tract of land in the Delaware River, turning it into the world's largest shipyard, able to build fifty ships at once. Shipyard workers were excused from the draft and their families allowed to hang service flags in their windows, as though they had family members in the armed forces. In a way they did, for shipyard work was dangerous; men were constantly being killed or hurt in accidents.

Shipbuilders copied the methods of Henry Ford, the automobile wizard. Cars, like every other machine, used to be built by skilled craftsmen, one at a time, from the ground up. Each individual piece of metal had to be cut and shaped by hand for its own special use. Ford, however, pioneered mass production and the assembly line. Each part was machine made to fit in the same place in all cars of a certain model. As the car body moved along the assembly line, workers added parts at their stations. Assembly line workers knew only how to do the simple task for which they'd been trained. It was like putting together a giant jigsaw puzzle, with each worker specializing in just one piece.

Americans discovered that Ford's methods could build ships as quickly as cars. Marine architects designed a certain type of vessel, then dozens were built, exactly alike, from factory-made parts. July 4, 1918, was a red-letter day. As the heroes of Belleau Wood paraded through Paris, ninety-five ships were launched at home.

In 1918, American shipyards built 533 ships, over three million tons, setting a world record for one year's production. They weren't very pretty ships, but they took to sea when the Allies needed them most.

France, Belgium, and Great Britain desperately needed food from overseas. With their young men at the front and large areas of their countries occupied, the first two couldn't grow enough to meet their needs. Great Britain, always a food importer, used every odd patch of land for crops. Grass to feed cattle was planted along railroad embankments; city parks were plowed up for vegetable gardens. Armies of children were released from school and, armed with hoes and shovels, marched into the countryside to help with the crops.

The United States became the Allies' breadbasket. Our country has been blessed with millions of acres of rich farmland. Throughout our history the American land has fed the American people and countless others besides.

A month after we went to war, Herbert Hoover was named chief of the United States Food Administration. A mining engineer by profession, Hoover was a skilled organizer who knew how to help others work together. After the war, he became the thirty-first President of the United States.

Hoover set out to educate Americans about the impor-

Herbert Hoover taught Americans how to "Hooverize," to save food in order to help the Allies.

tance of food. His slogan, "Food Will Win the War," followed them everywhere. It appeared on billboards in letters a yard high. Teachers drummed it into their classes; naughty youngsters stayed after school to copy it until their fingers ached. Mothers pointed to it on the dining room wall, neatly printed and framed, next to papa's or uncle's picture in uniform.

Our first task, Hoover explained, was to save food. This didn't mean eating less, but wasting less. He called this "food conservation," but the millions who followed his lead spoke of "Hooverizing." A true American Hooverized. Housewives didn't overload plates at mealtimes. Children were reminded to "chew your food" and "wipe your plate clean" to please the somber-faced Mr. Hoover. "Do not permit your child," said *Life* magazine, "to take a bite or two from an apple and throw the rest away; nowadays even children must be taught to be patriotic to the core." At Hoover's urging, the nation observed wheatless Mondays and Wednesdays, meatless Tuesdays, and porkless Thursdays and Saturdays.

The nation's second goal was to grow more food for export. Hoover encouraged farmers to bring every acre of their land under cultivation. They needn't worry about flooding the market and lowering prices; every grain of wheat, every ear of corn, was guaranteed to be sold at top dollar.

Youngsters in farm areas suddenly found that the war effort needed them as much as their older brothers and cousins. In the Northwest, high school boys over sixteen were released to help plant the 1918 spring wheat crop. Their reward came not in dollars, but in full credit for the school term.

City-dwellers learned farming skills. "The Hoe Behind

the Flag—Plant a Victory Garden," said a Food Administration slogan. Backyards and vacant lots sprouted into Victory Gardens, small farms to provide a family with its daily vegetables. Boy Scouts and Girl Scouts "adopted" Allied children; every pound of food they grew made available another pound to be shipped overseas. Even President Wilson got into the act. At his order, the White House lawn was turned into a Victory Garden supervised by the First Lady. When White House gardeners were released for war work, a flock of sheep took their place. These living lawn mowers trimmed the grass with their teeth and fertilized the soil with their manure. Mrs. Wilson later had the sheep sheared and their wool sold at auction for the benefit of the American Red Cross.

Hoover's program succeeded. Grain for making bread increased from under three and a half million tons before the war to nearly eleven million tons within a year. Meat and fats, so necesary for good health and work, skyrocketed from 640,000 tons to almost three and a half million tons. Without American food, the Allied peoples couldn't have kept up war production in their factories. Lack of food, as we'll see, was an important reason for the collapse of Germany's home front in the fall of 1918.

The First World War gave America's "left-outs" a chance to better their lives. When the war began, most blacks lived in the South as low-paid farmhands and unskilled laborers. The draft, however, created a labor shortage that had to be met quickly.

Northern factories acted as magnets, drawing blacks by the hundreds of thousands. Singly or in family groups, they settled in New York, St. Louis, Cleveland, Detroit, Chicago, and scores of smaller cities. There they found discrimination, even race riots in which people were burned out of their homes and sometimes killed.

Yet they also found opportunities they'd never known before. Factory wages were higher than farm wages; schools were better; talented people could rise above poverty more easily. The war opened a door for blacks that would never close. It was from then on that a civil rights movement grew and black citizens began to refuse to settle for less than complete equality with other Americans.

Women also gained ground because of the war. In America, as in Europe, women were still second-class citizens in many ways. Women, making up over half the population, couldn't vote in national elections. Scores of occupations were closed to them, not by law but by custom and prejudice. Building and repairing delicate machinery was man's work. Only men drove buses, sat at the throttle of locomotives, unloaded ships, delivered the mail, ran elevators, and worked telegraph keys. Most telephone operators were men, as were nearly all doctors, judges, and lawyers. When women did the same tasks as men, they seldom received equal pay for equal work.

In the same way that the war created opportunities for blacks, it opened a new world for women. The labor shortage brought women into jobs that nobody could have imagined a few years before. German women did heavy construction, working with pick and shovel to dig ditches, pave streets, and build the Berlin subway. French women became factory workers, gardeners, and letter carriers.

English women did *everything*. They filled every wartime job at home and at the front, except actual combat duty. They drove trucks, swept streets, carried sacks of coal on their backs, delivered milk cans and vegetables in crates, and

lugged baggage in railroad stations. Land-girls did the work
of able-bodied farmers.

Women practically took over Great Britain's war industries. Teenage girls, with their nimble, sensitive fingers, made
nearly all the fuses for artillery shells. "Munitionettes" filled
shell casings with high explosives. The unlucky ones were
called "yellow girls," because TNT dust turned their skin
a bright mustardy-yellow. Those who worked in poison gas
plants often became ill, or died from exposure to these
chemicals.

War work was especially hard for married women with
families to care for at home and husbands away at the front.
These women actually held down two full-time jobs. A
twelve-hour factory shift is tiring enough, without coming
home to more hours of household chores and child care.

Their sisters in uniform, however, lived with the sound of
the guns. Great Britain had an alphabet soup of women's
service units at the front. WAACs of the Women's Army
Auxiliary Corps worked in army offices, drove staff cars,
and generally made themselves useful. FANYs of the First
Aid Nursing Yeomanry drove ambulances from battlefield
dressing stations to base hospitals, often along roads plowed
by shellfire. During Ludendorff's 1918 offensive in Belgium,
FANYs evacuated over ten thousand wounded in eight days
and nights. VADs of the Voluntary Aid Detachment worked
with the British Red Cross, aiding the regular nurses as best
they could. Vera Britain recalled her VAD experiences during the Battle of the Lys:

> Gazing half-hypnotized at the disheveled beds, the stretchers
> on the floor, the scattered boots and piles of muddy khaki,
> the brown blankets turned back from smashed limbs bound

in splints by filthy blood-stained bandages . . . beneath each stinking wad of sodden wool and gauze an obscene horror waited for me, and all the equipment I had for attacking it was one pair of forceps standing in a . . . glass half-full of methylated spirit . . . the enemy within shelling distance, refugee sisters crowding in with nerves all awry . . . gassed men on stretchers, clawing the air—dying men reeking with mud and foul green-stained bandages . . . dead men with fixed empty eyes and shiny yellow faces. . . .

American women did the same kind of work as their European sisters, except for the backbreaking tasks such as ditch-

A British poster encouraging women to sign up for work in a munitions factory. Without women workers, it would have been impossible to produce the shells needed by the artillery at the front.

An American Red Cross worker serves hot chocolate to a soldier near the front.

digging. Not that they were being pampered; our labor shortage, though severe, was nothing like Europe's, so that these tasks could still be done by men. Nevertheless, women worked in munitions factories and other industries. Lady letter carriers appeared in cities, and Washington, D.C., had policewomen to direct traffic. Those who worked on the land were called "farmerettes."

Women who didn't hold full-time jobs helped the war effort in countless ways. Mothers and daughters joined knitting parties to make scarves and gloves for soldiers. Ladies' clubs rolled bandages. Housewives saved cooking fats, which were later converted into chemicals for explosives.

Those women who crossed the Big Pond to France belonged to the Army and Navy Nurse Corps and to various civilian service organizations: YMCA, American Red Cross, Salvation Army. The Navy and Marine Corps also recruited thousands of women as telephone operators, typists, and stenographers. These women wore uniforms and had full military rank, which meant that lower-ranking men had to salute them.

The Doughboys admired these hardworking women, but they loved Elsie Janis, the "Sweetheart of the AEF." Elsie, a star of Broadway musical comedy, did more than anyone else to entertain the troops in France. It was her own idea and she came as a private citizen, working without pay. Her mission in life, she believed, was to cheer the troops by bringing them a little bit of home. It also helped her forget the sorrow of having her fiancé killed in action.

Elsie Janis, "The Sweetheart of the AEF," entertains Americans of the First Division as they arrived at Washington Square, First Division Parade, New York City.

Fightingmen—Yanks, Englishmen, Canadians, Australians, New Zealanders, South Africans—gladly trudged through the mud to attend her performances. She'd appear anywhere, in town halls, tents, open fields. Elsie would step on stage and, without a microphone, ask, "Are we downhearted?" The "NO!" that boomed back at her sounded like a score of Big Berthas.

She kept going nonstop with acrobatics, impersonations, stories about home, and jokes about the "brass hats," conceited officers. Her songs were snappy and cheerful, like Elsie herself. The soldiers' favorites were "It's a Long Way to Berlin (*But we'll get there*)," "Oh, You Dirty Germans (*We wish the same to you*)," and "All We Do Is Sign the Payroll (*And we never see a cent*)." She always ended with her own version of "Over There," called "Over Here." Elsie even got a laugh out of Black Jack Pershing, whom she called "Boss General."

The First World War changed not only the way women worked, but how they looked and lived. Before the war, American and European women wore high-necked, tight-fitting dresses with hems that swept the ground; showing one's ankles was considered disgraceful except at the bathing beach. Hair often reaching to the waist, was piled in a huge bun on top of the head and crowned by wide-brimmed feathered hats held in place with dagger-length pins.

This style went out with the war, never to return. Women's clothes had to become simpler, more practical, if they were to share in the war effort. Long dresses actually became dangerous in factories, around whirring machinery; besides, they used up scarce cloth. Long hair was hot and uncomfortable, while pins wasted steel needed for guns. As a result, dresses became shorter; indeed, daring younger women gave them up in favor of pants. Lightweight, easy-to-move-in and safer around machinery, pants quickly became fashionable; they have been popular ever since. So has short hair, which is easier to comb and keep clean.

War work also made women more independent. A steady job meant money of one's own to spend, without having to explain or apologize to anyone. For the first time large numbers of women earned enough to support themselves and to live their own lives as they pleased. The war, explained one woman in her mid-twenties, brought "blessed freedom," giving her a chance "to be as free as a man."

Finally, American and most European women gained the right to vote in the 1920s. After their services in the war, few could deny that they'd *earned* equality with men. War, in its own strange way, had brought some good out of evil.

Winning the war on the home front meant winning people's hearts and minds. Government is powerful, but power can't do everything, especially in a democracy, where leaders are elected. President Wilson simply couldn't order people to work and sacrifice for the war effort. To get the most out of them, they had to *believe* in the Allied cause and *want* to do their best for it.

Helping them to believe and want to help was the propagandist's job. The propagandist is a communications expert. Unlike the teacher or the journalist, whose aim is to inform people by telling the truth, his aim is to persuade them to believe in a certain way and act on their beliefs. It makes no difference how he achieves his aims, so long as he succeeds. He may tell lies, hoping they'll never be discovered or discovered when it doesn't matter anymore. Usually, though, he prefers to tell the truth, shaping it and slanting it to get his message across. Modern nations, including democracies, always use propaganda in war. Whether their cause is good or bad, propaganda helps keep their people's loyalty while weakening their opponent's cause.

American propaganda during the First World War was directed by a well-known newspaperman named George Creel. A week after we declared war on Germany, the President named Creel to head the Committee on Public Information. As Creel saw it, the war was "a plain publicity proposition . . . the world's greatest adventure in salesmanship." His mission was to sell the war to the American people and keep them sold on it.

Creel was a tireless worker who always seemed to be inventing new ways of selling the war. Among these ways were the Four-Minute Men. The original Minute Men had fought for American independence with muskets; Creel's warriors used words. Seventy-five thousand men were recruited to give four-minute speeches on war-related subjects. At first they spoke at intermissions at movie theaters on topics such as "Why We Are Fighting" and "What Our Real Enemy

George Creel of the Committee on Public Information was the nation's propaganda chief, responsible for "selling" the war to the American people.

Is." Before long, you couldn't attend a public gathering without having to sit through a lecture. No ballpark crowd was too large, no church social too small, to escape a visit from Creel's speakers.

Even God was dragged into the war effort. Depending upon where you heard it, God was American, British, or French. German soldiers had a motto in raised letters on their belt buckles: "*Gott mit uns*": "God with us."

The Committee on Public Information also hired advertising men to mass-produce slogans. A slogan is a catchphrase, short and snappy, that helps people remember without really thinking. There was a lot to remember during the First World War, and slogans changed as quickly as the needs of the war effort.

Slogan-makers had a field day with the Liberty Loan drives. War is a nation's most costly activity. From the moment we declared war on Germany until her surrender, the government spent at least two million dollars *an hour*. Part of this immense cost came from taxes, the rest from borrowing. Again and again the American people were asked to take part in the Liberty Loans, to help pay for the war by buying bonds.

Slogans drummed out the message that buying bonds was a citizen's duty: "Buy Bonds Till it Hurts." Anyone who didn't buy bonds, or didn't buy enough, was made to feel disloyal. Such people were letting our boys down and helping the enemy: "The Soldier Gives—You Must Lend," "A Bond Slacker is a Kaiser Backer."

One aim of war propaganda is to stir hatred and fear of the enemy through atrocity stories. Atrocities are war crimes, deliberate cruelty toward prisoners, wounded, and civilians; the unnecessary destruction of works of art and houses of worship are also war crimes. Whenever armies have fought, there have always been some who committed atrocities.

During the First World War, individual Allied soldiers, Yanks included, violated the laws of war. German machine gunners who fought to the last moment before surrendering were occasionally shot as they raised their hands. Rather than expose themselves to sniper fire, Allied troops sometimes "lost" prisoners they'd been detailed to escort to the rear.

Yet these acts were nowhere as frequent or as awful as German propaganda claimed. Germans told wild tales of prisoners being blinded by their Allied captors. A Belgian priest was accused of hiding a machine gun behind a church altar to shoot German troops at prayer. French nurses were said to poison German wounded. These and similar stories were told, and believed, in Germany. We know today that these were made up by propagandists who never came within miles of the front.

Germans, however, were guilty of some serious atrocities. The kaiser's army followed a deliberate policy of *Schreck-lichkeit*—frightfulness—against civilians, especially in Belgium early in the war. If snipers fired on passing troops from houses in a town, the town was burned, innocent and guilty suffering alike. Sometimes, as at Termonde and Dinant, scores of hostages were executed if townspeople didn't turn in a sniper. Louvain, famous for its university and church dating from the Middle Ages, was destroyed in reprisal for snipers. The great cathedral of Reims, France, was used as an aiming point by German artillery spotters.

The German record was bad enough, but not as bad as Allied propagandists said. Horrible stories were invented about how Germans crucified prisoners with bayonets through the hands and feet. Airmen were accused of showering France with deadly "gifts" for children, such as poisoned candy and toys that exploded when wound up. Propagandists charged that the Germans were such monsters that they gathered bodies from the battlefield, tied them into bundles, and sent them home to be made into fertilizer and soap. These stories were as false as any made up in Berlin.

Creel, who believed a picture is worth a thousand words, brought the nation's artists into the propaganda war. Through the Division of Pictorial Publicity, painters, illustrators, and cartoonists shocked the nation with terrifying images. Their works showed the Germans not as human beings, but as hulking, drooling beasts. Their purpose was to frighten people into believing that the enemy was a born criminal who enjoyed causing pain.

Cartoonists drew crying children, their hands cut off by lunatic Germans, who also tossed infants into the air and caught them on bayonets. One cartoonist showed a soldier marching with his rifle over his shoulder; infants are skewered on the bayonet, like meat at a barbecue. War is the father of lies. And during the First World War many people felt that any lie was good if it persuaded others to work their hardest for victory.

Creel was proudest of his poster artists. Advertising with posters used to be big business, before radio and television. To be effective, a poster had to be simple and colorful, with a striking picture and little or no text. It was this simplicity and boldness that made posters valuable for propaganda. A few of these posters are works of great beauty and may be seen in art museums today.

You couldn't escape propaganda posters in wartime America. Wherever you went, in trains, on the street, in school, you were surrounded by posters varying in size from that of a sheet of notebook paper to a billboard occupying three hundred square feet. Some made simple requests: "SAVE FOOD," "BUY COAL EARLY," "FATS ARE NEEDED." Recruiting posters encouraged men to enlist in the services, rather than wait to be drafted. "I WANT YOU—FOR THE NAVY," says a beautiful girl in a sailor suit. "GEE!! I WISH I WERE A MAN— I'D JOIN THE NAVY," echoes another poster queen.

Liberty Loan posters warned that we must "HALT THE HUN!" in Europe, otherwise he'd repeat his atrocities here. Other posters shout "REMEMBER BELGIUM" and "BEAT BACK THE HUN WITH LIBERTY BONDS." One poster shows German planes flying over New York Harbor. The water and sky are orange, reflecting the flames of the burning city. The Statue of Liberty, headless, her torch lying at her feet, stands wrapped in fire. The caption warns, "THAT LIBERTY SHALL NOT PERISH FROM THE EARTH—BUY LIBERTY BONDS."

Creel had a valuable helper in the young movie industry. Moving pictures, which were invented in 1894 by Thomas A. Edison, lent themselves to war propaganda. Although films were still silent, their flickering black and white images made the war real for millions of civilians. For the first time in history, war became immediate, an experience to be felt far from the battlefields.

Propaganda films poured out of Hollywood. Like posters, they showed the enemy as totally evil, the Allies as pure and good. They included heroic epics such as *Pershing's Crusaders* and *To Hell with the Kaiser*, as well as horror films with hair-raising titles: *The Claws of the Hun* and *The Kaiser—The Beast of Berlin*. These showed how Germans mistreated children, murdered innocents, and raised flies that carried disease germs on their feet. In *The Little American*, Mary Pickford played a golden-haired orphan wandering

I WANT YOU

for THE NAVY

OMOTION FOR ANY ONE ENLISTING
PPLY ANY RECRUITING STATION
OR POSTMASTER

Beat back the HUN
with
LIBERTY BONDS

THAT LIBERTY SHALL NOT
PERISH FROM THE EARTH
BUY LIBERTY BONDS
FOURTH   LIBERTY   LOAN

across no-man's-land and falling into the clutches of the horrible Hun.

War films changed the way American children played. Boys gave up Cowboys and Indians in favor of Over the Top and Hunt the Hun, the object being to make the enemy shout *Kamerad!* Girls played Red Cross Nurse, caring for "wounded" dolls and small brothers.

Hours before President Wilson delivered his war message, he told a friend something that had been troubling him for a long time. "Once lead this people into war," he said, "and they'll forget there ever was such a thing as tolerance. To fight you must be brutal and ruthless, and the spirit of ruthless brutality will . . . infect Congress, the courts, the policeman on the beat, the man in the street." His greatest fear was that the United States Constitution, the foundation stone of our liberties, couldn't survive a total war. Free speech would vanish, along with the other freedoms Americans enjoy. We would become no better than our enemies.

The President understood that a country at war is like a chain under terrific strain. Just as a chain is only as strong as its weakest link, a nation's strength depends upon the cooperation of its people. To question the war's justice, to persuade others that it is wrong, and to refuse to work for victory weakens the home front. And weakness brings defeat. Thus it is difficult to safeguard civil liberties when nations are fighting for their lives.

President Wilson's fears soon proved justified. The war to make the world safe for democracy was a harsh test of democratic principles. A wave of hatred of all things German swept the country. Hundreds of thousands of loyal Americans became victims of bigotry simply because they spoke German or their ancestors had come from Germany. Much of this bigotry was plain silliness. German measles was renamed "liberty measles," while sauerkraut became "liberty cabbage." Dachshunds were turned into "liberty pups," and hamburger dubbed "Salisbury steak."

Anti-German feeling, however, quickly took a dangerous turn. Shopkeepers with German-sounding names had their windows broken by mobs. Libraries burned their German books. Universities canceled courses in the German language and literature. Record shops took music by German composers off their shelves. Dr. Karl Muck, conductor of the Boston Symphony Orchestra, was arrested for playing German music. The patriotic mayor of Jersey City, New Jersey, helped win the war by refusing to allow Austrian-born violinist Fritz Kreisler to play at a concert. The Montana State Council ordered schools to stop using a history text thought too favorable to the Germans before the year 812 A.D. German-born office workers were fired as security risks, although their sons were with General Pershing overseas.

Americans had reason to be concerned about security. People remembered the Black Tom explosion and didn't want it repeated now that we were in the war. Congress replied with the Espionage and Sedition Acts, laws to prevent the weakening of the war effort by word or deed. A person could get into trouble for interfering with the draft, saying anything to harm the sale of Liberty Bonds, or speaking against the government or armed forces. Violators might be fined ten thousand dollars and sent to prison for twenty years.

The police and courts took these laws seriously. One man was jailed for laughing at draftees. Magazines and newspapers critical of the war were kept out of the United States mails. A film producer was sent to prison for ten years. His crime: making *The Spirit of '76* showing Thomas Jefferson signing the Declaration of Independence and Redcoats bayoneting patriots. No one denied that these events happened during the Revolution; only showing them in a movie now was criminal because it might stir anger against our British ally.

Before long, the twin epidemics of "spy fever" and "U-boat jitters" gripped the nation. People constantly poked into one another's business, eager to detect spies. A street conversation in German might bring a visit from the police and some hard questions. The governor of Ohio ordered that only English was to be spoken in public, including houses of worship. "Let those who cannot speak or understand the English language," he added, "conduct their religious worship in their homes." Members of patriotic organizations kept a lookout for "gloaters," those who seemed to enjoy news of German victories. In short, busybodies, tattletales, and gossipers had a grand time during the First World War.

People along the seacoasts went in fear of submarines. The summer of 1918 was an especially bad time. On July 19, the cruiser *San Diego* struck a submarine-laid mine off Fire Island, New York, losing six sailors. Two days later the U-156 surfaced off Orleans on Cape Cod, Massachusetts. With hundreds of vactioners looking on, she shelled passing boats until driven off by planes from a nearby naval air station. Altogether, U-boats sank seventy-nine vessels off our Atlantic coast.

Submarines certainly were a problem, but not as serious as people imagined. The undersea raiders were spotted every-where; indeed, more were seen in one day than the German navy had cruising in all the oceans of the world. Pleasure boats reported periscopes and torpedo trails from Canada to Florida. One sighting was made in the Great Lakes! Americans became so jittery that the most innocent act might bring suspicion of spying or signaling to U-boats. People were arrested for keeping a lamp lit at night, or when the sun's rays flashed on a shaving mirror, near a window within sight of the sea. Yet nobody was ever found guilty of signaling the kaiser's submarines.

One didn't have to be a traitor to be against the First World War. There were law-abiding, patriotic Americans who believed their country had no business interfering in a foreign conflict. Europe's war was Europe's affair, they said. Neither the Allies nor the Central Powers cared about democracy, only about gaining colonies and protecting the profits of munitions manufacturers. Ordinary Americans had no stake in this war but were, rather, its victims. If Europeans wanted to fight, let them do so with their own sons, not ours.

Opponents denounced the war at every opportunity. Several labor unions, notably the IWW (International Workers of the World), held antiwar demonstrations. The Woman's Peace Party was organized to protest American participation. Among its leaders were Jane Addams, a famous social worker, and Crystal Eastman, a lawyer interested in women's rights cases. Helen Keller, the blind and deaf author and lecturer, condemned the war as a gigantic waste of blood and treasure. For a time the song "I Didn't Raise My Boy to Be a Soldier" was popular among women.

Certain people saw the draft as the destroyer of America's youth. The draft made soldiers, and Eugene V. Debs of the American Socialist Party believed soldiers were mindless robots trained to kill for a few cents a day. "War," he thundered, "is a crimson carnival where the drunken devils are unchained and snarling dogs are 'sicked' upon one another . . . [to] shoot off one another's heads [and] rip open one another's bellies."

Thousands of Americans were offended by such talk. Their loved ones were with the AEF and they knew they weren't "snarling dogs." The government, too, resented these criticisms, for they might undermine faith in the Allied cause, bringing defeat. As a result, the Woman's Peace Party magazine was banned from the mails. Debs was sentenced to ten years in prison, although he received a pardon after the war. IWW offices were raided by the police and their leaders given long prison terms.

Although troubled by many problems, the American home front was heaven compared to war-torn Europe. In Great Britain, France, and Germany antiwar publications were not just kept out of the mails, but shut down entirely. Antiwar rallies were broken up by club-swinging police or mobs of soldiers on leave. French conscientious objectors, men who refused to fight because they believed killing was sinful, were shot and their relatives sent a short telegram: "Died a coward!" The Muslim majority in Turkey butchered two million Armenian Christians, claiming they were disloyal to the Central Powers.

Nothing like these horrors took place in the United States. The Founding Fathers, had they returned in 1918, would have been proud of their handiwork. For despite the pressures of total war, despite even the wrongs done hundreds of individuals, our Constitution held firm. The United States emerged from the war years as she'd entered them: a democracy devoted to the rule of law.

SIX

Aces High

★ The wish to fly is as old as humanity. People have always admired the birds, envied them, and hoped one day to imitate them. "Free as a bird," we say, as if freedom and flight are the same. Our word *aviation* comes from the Latin *avis*, bird; an "aviator" is a birdman.

As the centuries passed, man did, indeed, learn to fly. In 1783, the year the American Revolution ended, the Mont-golfier brothers in France discovered lighter-than-air flight using balloons. These were merely enormous cloth bags filled with heated air, and later helium gas, that drifted on the air currents. Count Ferdinand von Zeppelin later perfected the dirigible, a cigar-shaped airship powered by motors. Al-though important, these developments were far from the dream of free, birdlike, flight. Balloons and dirigibles were slow, forced either to move in the direction of the wind or unable to resist strong headwinds. Only heavier-than-air flight in airplanes would make man truly the rival of the birds.

The airplane, or aeroplane, is just what its name says: a machine kept airborne by means of flat surfaces—planes or wings—and driven by propellers or jet engines. The airplane age began at 10:35 A.M., Thursday, December 17, 1903, on the beach at Kitty Hawk, North Carolina. On that morning the *Flyer*, a plane built by Orville and Wilbur Wright, bicycle mechanics from Dayton, Ohio, amazed onlookers at a nearby Coast Guard station. With Orville lying flat on the lower of *Flyer*'s two wings, it rose into the air and moved under its own power for twelve seconds, a distance of four hundred twenty feet.

The Wright brothers' invention was soon copied, and improved upon, by aviation pioneers in America and Europe. Daredevil pilots risked their lives testing new models; often the planes failed the tests, breaking their pilots' necks. Nevertheless, planes grew steadily more powerful and airworthy.

"We thought," said Orville of these heroic days, "we were introducing into the world an invention which would make future wars practically impossible." Seldom has so intelligent a person been so wrong about something so important.

What the airplane really did was to make wars more terrible. Within a few years of Kitty Hawk, nations were creating air services to experiment with the military uses of aviation. In October 1911, Italy became the first to use aircraft in war. During its war with Turkey, a pilot flew over enemy lines in Tripoli, North Africa, to observe troop movements. Other Italian pilots "bombed" the enemy with stones and grenades. The British approach was more scientific. By 1913 they'd flown planes from ships' decks, air-dropped torpedoes, and tracked submarines from aloft.

Airplanes appeared over the Western Front early in the

First World War. Flimsy, unarmed craft, they were not meant to fight; when the war began, no nation had planes built specially to fight other planes. Their only purpose was scouting, spying on enemy movements and photographing his positions. Whenever Allied and German planes crossed paths in flight, the pilots waved and went about their business. They couldn't do anything else without weapons.

Such pleasantness couldn't last long. Aircraft were becoming the eyes of the ground forces. Without their reports, commanders groped in the dark, unable to form an accurate picture of enemy strengths and abilities. It therefore became necessary for each side to destroy the other's observation planes while protecting its own.

This was easier said than done. Knocking down airplanes proved to be a difficult task, especially from the ground. Try throwing a stone at a butterfly in midair and you'll have an idea of the problems involved. Troops blazed away with rifles and machine guns, wasting millions of bullets without hitting their target. And when they did, it was due more to luck than skill.

The best way to shoot down a plane is to fire at it from another plane. Flyers began taking potshots at the enemy with pistols and rifles. In two-seater aircraft, a marksman sat behind the pilot with a machine gun mounted on a swivel stand. Still it took a steady hand and keen eyesight to hit the mark. Usually the aircraft's own vibrations combined with the wind's blast to spoil the shooter's aim. Gunners succeeded in destroying a few enemy planes, but for the most part the results weren't worth the bother.

The only solution was to fix a machine gun firmly to the plane's hood in front of the pilot, who'd fire it straight ahead. In effect, the entire aircraft became a gun aimed along the pilot's line of sight. It was a sensible idea, except that the propeller kept getting in the way. After a few bursts, the bullets sawed through the propeller blades, flinging debris backward into the pilot's face. The propellerless craft then plunged earthward out of control.

Military aviation had reached a dead end when Anthony Fokker, a Dutch engineer who built planes in Germany, tackled the problem. Born in 1890, Fokker had loved machinery since childhood. As a schoolboy, he'd invented a cheating machine that gave him test answers quickly and safely, under the teachers' very noses.

Fokker's latest invention was more dangerous. He remembered how, as a child in Holland, he'd tossed rocks between the moving vanes of windmills; it was just a matter of timing, of deciding when the stone would miss the giant blades. Timing was also the key to passing bullets through a whirring propeller.

During two days' work in 1915, Fokker invented the interrupter gear to do just that. The gear was attached to the propeller and to a machine gun trigger in such a way that, whenever a blade moved in front of the gun, its firing was interrupted for an instant. Thus the propeller controlled the gun, saving itself from destruction. The interrupter gear gave birth to the fighter plane, and with it to full-scale war in the sky.

German fighters equipped with Fokker's invention ruled Europe's skies. Allied airmen were helpless against the device. "Fokker Fodder" they called themselves, meat for Germany's sky wolves.

Just when it seemed that the Fokkers owned the sky, the Allies' luck changed. German pilots had been ordered not to fly over Allied territory for fear of being downed with the interrupter gear aboard. That fear proved justified when a pilot lost his bearings in a fog several weeks later. As the needle of his fuel gauge teetered over empty, he saw lights flickering through a break in the clouds. When his plane skidded to a stop moments later, he found himself on a French airfield. Pilot, plane, and interrupter gear were captured. After studying the gear, the Allies "borrowed" the idea for their own planes. The race was on.

During the years that followed, both sides struggled to create better and better fighters. Each nation had its favorites. Germany set the pace with its Fokker, Albatros, Pfalz, Taub, and Aviatik fighters. The French challenged them with the Nieuport and Spad, later favored by the Americans. Great Britain took pride in the Sopwith Camel and De Havilland DH-4, a scout-fighter-bomber rolled into one. Soon the pure bomber appeared. Britain's Handley-Pages and Germany's Gothas and Zeppelins were forerunners of the bomber fleets of the Second World War.

Yet it was the fighter that dominated the air over the Western Front. This was still a primitive machine, slow, delicate, and deadly. There were three basic designs according to the number of wings. Monoplanes, biplanes, and triplanes had one, two, and three sets of wings; in biplanes and triplanes the extra wings, arranged one above the other and supported by wooden posts, gave the craft added stability in flight.

Everything possible was done to save weight. The plane's body was a wooden skeleton held together with steel wire. This skeleton was covered by a canvas skin coated with "dope," a highly flammable varnish. Repairs were made with wire clippers, scissors, and glue.

The pilot sat in an open cockpit, exposed to the elements.

Dressed in a fur-lined flight suit, he braved the high-altitude cold; some men flew with bottles of whiskey to help keep them warm. When it rained, the pilot became soaked to the skin, the water sloshing around on the cockpit floor as the plane rolled from side to side. His seat, made of flammable wicker, rested above the gasoline tank and fuel lines leading to the engine. It was like riding a bomb, while holding another bomb in your lap.

First World War fighters weighed between twelve hundred and two thousand pounds, could climb to twenty thousand feet, and travel between seventy and one hundred thirty miles an hour. Most could stay aloft less than three and a half hours. The usual armament was two forward-firing machine guns. The German machine gun had a trick-name, the Parabellum. It came from the Latin proverb, "If you want peace, prepare for war"—*para bellum* (for war). German airmen thought of their machine gun as frontier marshals thought of their six-shooters: they were "peacemakers."

These fighters of the First World War were toys compared to modern jets. The United States Air Force's F-15 Eagle, for example, weighs forty thousand pounds, can fight at sixty thousand feet, and flies at Mach 2.5+, that is, over two and a half times the speed of sound, better than two thousand miles an hour. Since the Eagle is faster than any machine gun bullet, its main armaments are missiles that home in on the enemy's heat trail. We've come a long way since Kitty Hawk.

In the First World War, airmen, regardless of nationality, had certain things in common. Sky-fighting was a young man's occupation. Pilots were mostly between the ages of nineteen and twenty-five. Older men are seldom as daring, nor are their reflexes as quick, their vision as sharp.

Sky-fighting was extremely dangerous, with no room for error. If you made a mistake, you died. Period. New pilots lasted an average of three weeks in combat over the Western Front. An airman knew the score when he enlisted; nobody forced him into a cockpit. Yet, to his mind, there was no contest between the flyer's life and the footsoldier's. The infantryman was part of a mass that took away his identity as a person. He dressed as others dressed, did as they did. His duty wasn't to think for himself, but to obey orders instantly, without questioning. Not the aviator. He was an individualist, a knight of the skies.

The knight of the Middle Ages looked down on the humble infantry from horseback. The modern knight flew over them in his airplane. They were the "PBI"—the Poor Bloody Infantry—wallowing in the slime and gore of the trenches. Unlike the PBI, the flyer chose his style of fighting. Once a dogfight began, he obeyed only his own orders. He alone decided how to attack, when to defend, where to retreat, betting his life on the choice.

Airmen weren't bound by the infantry's drab uniform. They designed their own outfits, which might include school sweaters, bearskin overcoats, tight breeches, and long scarves that trailed behind in the breeze. Pets, including wolfhounds and monkeys, often shared the cockpit.

Planes were as colorful as their pilots. Each squadron, often each man in a squadron, selected its own color arrangements. The Canadian Black Squadron resembled a fleet of airborne pirate ships. Decked out in patterns of black and white, with grinning skulls painted on the wings, the planes had such names as *Black Sheep*, *Black Maria*, and *Black Roger*—from Jolly Roger, the pirates' skull-and-crossbones flag. France's dreaded Stork Squadrons shimmered in metallic yellows and greens, with the stork emblem painted below the cockpit.

Life, while it lasted, was as comfortable as could be expected in a world war. Pilots slept in clean beds, ate hot food, and drank whiskey—plenty of whiskey. Servants, called batmen, cleaned their quarters and cared for their belongings.

If you survived, you were considered a special person. The Allies called anyone who downed at least five enemy planes an "ace," after the high card of the deck. Germany's champions were *Kanone*—cannon—or "big shots."

Top-scorers were treated as today's sports and rock music stars. Civilians were interested in the smallest details of their lives: their favorite foods, how they dressed, their wives and girlfriends. Fans followed them everywhere, begging for autographs. Little boys recited the dates of their victories and the types of planes downed, as if they were batting averages.

Some aces became legends, remembered until our own day. Captain Oswald Boelcke, one of Germany's finest pilots, was a softspoken, kindly man who prayed for his victims' souls until he joined them in death after forty victories. Britain's Captain Albert Ball, with forty-four victories by age twenty, hated war and tried to forget its horrors by playing the violin—until his luck run out.

Air combat was always painful for Captain Georges Guynemer, one of France's leading aces with fifty-two victories. Guynemer, small and frail, suffered from tuberculosis. High-altitude flying and steep dives tore at his weakened lungs like eagle claws. He constantly coughed up globs of blood. Yet he fought his sickness as fiercely as he fought the enemy until the day he disappeared. French schoolchildren said their hero flew so high that God decided to keep him.

Captain Werner Voss was a happy-go-lucky fellow who downed forty-eight enemies for the kaiser. On September 23,

1917, Voss fought one of the greatest air battles on record. During a one-man patrol, he sighted a formation of twenty British fighters. Without hesitating, he dived his checkered Fokker straight into the enemy formation. For a half-hour he cut and weaved, rolled and banked, until they sent him earthward in flames.

Voss's countryman was Baron Manfred von Richthofen, the First World War's leading ace. Richthofen, cold and distant, with no close friends, enjoyed killing. When off duty, he'd slip into a forest with a rifle for a few hours' hunting. But the thrill of the hunt was nothing to the thrill of killing men. Richthofen took pleasure in blasting enemies out of the sky.

You could have picked Richthofen out of a skyful of planes. Nicknamed the Red Baron, he flew to battle in a blood-red Fokker triplane. His squadron was known as the Flying Circus, because its planes were painted in loud colors,

Baron Manfred von Richthofen, Germany's "Red Baron," destroyed eighty Allied aircraft before being shot down by a British pilot. The medal he is wearing is the Prussian Order of Merit, known as the "Blue Max" because of its blue ribbon.

like circus wagons. An Allied pilot remembered "machines with green wings and yellow noses, silver wings and gold noses, red bodies with green wings, light blue bodies with red wings." The Red Baron was killed after scoring eighty victories.

Some Americans became aces nearly a year before their country joined the Allies. These were the pilots of the Lafayette Escadrille, or squadron, which was part of a larger grouping called the Lafayette Flying Corps.

The war was only hours old when Americans began to volunteer for the French Foreign Legion as infantrymen. The Allies, they believed, were fighting in a just cause, one Americans should be proud to serve. Yet, as Americans, they couldn't swear allegiance to another country without losing their citizenship. The Foreign Legion offered a way out, because it required no oath of loyalty to France, only a promise to obey orders faithfully. Once in the Foreign Legion they joined men from many nations: Poles, Russians, Spaniards, Greeks, Mexicans, Arabs, Chinese, Norwegians, Danes, Swedes. Eight hundred Germans and Austrians living in France offered to fight their native countries. Their pay was thirty cents a month.

Hundreds of Americans saw action with the Foreign Legion during the next two years. Among them were several with flying experience; others were eager to become pilots to escape the trenches. By 1916 these men, plus others recruited in the United States, were accepted for training as fighter pilots. Those who passed the course joined French squadrons. But whatever their squadron, they belonged to the Lafayette Flying Corps composed of Americans in the French air service.

A number of their comrades, however, formed the Lafayette Escadrille, an all-American squadron. Their insignia
was as American as it could be: the head of an Indian chief in
war paint wearing a feathered war bonnet. The French
people learned to love that emblem. No Frenchman would
accept money from anyone who wore it, regardless of the
purchase. It was a matter of honor with them; for these Yanks
had volunteered to serve France and it would have been
rude to take their money when they offered their lives freely.

Lafayette Escadrille members were a rugged bunch who'd
do anything to fly for the Allies. William Thaw, an amateur
pilot who'd flown under New York's East River bridges, was
blind in one eye. No matter. During his medical examination
Thaw fooled the doctor by reading the eye chart twice with
his good eye, scoring a perfect 20/20 for both eyes. His
comrade, Bert Hall, knew nothing about airplanes, but that
didn't stop him from claiming to be an experienced airman.
When an officer dared him to prove it, he leaped into the
cockpit of a Nieuport and revved the engine. Instantly the
plane moved down the field like a weaving drunkard and
lurched into the air. Men dove for cover as the runaway
buzzed the field, finally crashing into a hangar. Hall, with
more luck than brains, staggered from the wreckage. "Why,
why," the officer sputtered, "you know nothing at all about
flying!" "No," Hall admitted, "but I thought I might be
able to get the hang of it." Fortunately the officer thought
that someone with such nerve might make a good pilot, so
Hall was sent to school to learn flying the right way. Both
Thaw and Hall became aces.

The Lafayette Escadrille's most famous member was Raoul
Gervais Lufbery, an American of French parentage from
Wallingford, Connecticut. Born in 1885, Lufbery was older

than most of his comrades. A short, stocky man with a bull-neck, he'd been a wanderer most of his life. Among his jobs were sailor, factory worker, and mechanic; he also did a hitch in the United States Army in the Philippines, becoming a crack shot with a rifle.

In Calcutta, India, he teamed up with Marc Pourpe, a French stunt flyer. Lufbery and Pourpe became almost like brothers, traveling throughout Asia and Africa. The natives were amazed at these "sky gods" come to earth. Pourpe joined the French air force when the war began, taking along Lufbery as his mechanic. When he was killed, Lufbery learned to fly to avenge his friend's death.

Lufbery took to flying as easily as a duckling to water. Always cool, always careful, he became the terror of the German squadrons near Verdun. His victories made him the Lafayette Escadrille's top ace, as well as America's first and greatest ace of the war. Although officially credited with only seventeen victories, fellow pilots saw him destroy at least forty enemies; to be credited, however, a kill had to be reported by friendly ground forces, impossible since he usually fought deep behind German lines.

The more he fought, the more he learned about fighting. He invented the Lubfery Circle, used by American fighter pilots until the 1950s. He knew from American history that pioneers had formed their wagons into circles to fight off Indian attacks; the circle allowed defenders to cover their position from all angles, all the time. Lufbery applied this lesson to air combat. Whenever he led a flight, the planes flew in a large circle, each covering the others to avoid nasty surprises. If the enemy appeared, they scattered for a dogfight, an every-man-for-himself battle at close quarters.

Lufbery was a celebrity both in France and the United

States. Crowds mobbed him, jostling for a chance to shake his hand. Mothers named their newborn babies after him. He received scores of letters from women admirers offering themselves to him in marriage. He remained a bachelor.

Lufbery never boasted or took credit for himself. His success, he said, was mostly luck, and no one should take credit for being lucky. He'd spend his off-duty hours romping with the squadron's mascots, two tame lions named Whiskey and Soda, or escaping to the quiet loneliness of the forest. He wandered the forest, thinking to himself and collecting mushrooms for the squadron's mess.

The Lafayette Flying Corps and Lafayette Escadrille lasted only as long as American neutrality. Once the United States joined the Allies, they became part of the AEF. They were a real prize. Overnight the United States gained battle-wise pilots proud of their record and able to pass on their wisdom to others.

It was an enviable record. American volunteers were credited with 199 victories, although they probably downed an equal number for which they weren't credited. Eleven Lafayette Escadrille flyers became aces.

Yet these victories came at a high price. Of the 224 Americans who flew for France, eleven died of illness or accident, fifteen became prisoners, and fifty-one died in combat; that's a casualty rate of 43 percent, about what the infantry suffered in the trenches. Lafayette flyers may have escaped the filth of the trenches, but not their dangers.

We were lucky to have the Lafayette Flying Corps, for we had nothing else capable of fighting in the sky. The nation that gave the world the airplane had surrendered its lead to others. Although the government bought some ex-

perimental planes from the Wright brothers and Glenn
Curtiss, builder of the first seaplane, it was unwilling to spend
more than a few thousand dollars on these newfangled
devices.

No major power did less for military aviation than the
United States. When war came in 1917, we were short of
everything that had to do with flying. There were only two
military airfields in the entire country: one borrowed from
an airplane company outside San Diego, California, the other
on Long Island, New York. There was no air force, only
the Aviation Section of the Signal Corps, the service branch
responsible for communications and photography.

The Aviation Section was laughable, compared to the air
services the Europeans had created. Its total strength was
sixty-five officers, including thirty-five pilots, and fewer
than eleven hundred enlisted men. It numbered three hundred training planes, none of which had a chance against a
real fighter. No American plane mounted machine guns. No
Aviation Section pilot had ever seen an air battle, let alone
participated in one. The United States of America owned
not a single combat plane.

The only American-built warplane to see action was the
De Havilland DH-4, manufactured in Detroit for the British.
Our DH-4s, however, were a disaster. Airmen hated these
"Flaming Coffins," so-called because of their habit of burst-
ing into flames due to defective fuel tanks.

No plane of American design ever fought in the First
World War. General Halsey Dunwoody, in charge of buying aviation supplies for the Army, said it all: "We never
had a single plane that was fit to use." Our airmen did their
fighting in Spads, Nieuports, and Camels borrowed from
the Allies.

But planes don't fly themselves; men fly them, and here we succeeded better than anyone expected. The Committee on Public Information began a campaign to recruit men for the Aviation Section, renamed the Air Service. Colorful posters appeared on college campuses, tempting young men to become "Eagles," to seek fame and adventure in the air.

Within eighteen months of declaring war, the United States had the makings of a mighty air force. In November 1918, the Air Service stood at two hundred thousand officers and men. Forty-five American squadrons, 750 planes, were at the front, with others forming. Training centers at home were turning out officers, mechanics, machine gunners, and armorers. Ten thousand cadets graduated from flight schools, where they'd learned the airman's basic skills.

The best cadets were sent to Europe for advanced training with combat planes. There was plenty to learn, since fighters were faster and more temperamental than "Jennies," the Curtiss JN-4 trainers they'd used in the States. The Spad, for example, was a bucking bronco; old-timers wore spurs in flight, just to show that this tiny terror couldn't throw them.

Flying wasn't a matter of sitting back and allowing the plane to carry you into battle. It was work—hard, exciting work that demanded concentration and coordination. Then, as now, a fighter's cockpit had a bewildering array of instruments. In it were a compass, airspeed indicator, radiator thermometer, altimeter, fuel gauge, and oil pressure indicator, plus a map case and drums of spare ammunition. Whatever else a pilot did, flying or fighting, he had to scan the instruments every few seconds to make sure everything was working normally. If they weren't, he'd better go home fast or find a clearing to set down in.

The pilot's hands were always full, his feet always busy. With the right hand he held the joystick, the steering lever, which moved in four directions. Pushing the joystick forward pointed the plane's nose down, sending it into a power-dive. Pulling it back brought up the nose, putting it into a climb; a sudden, sharp-angled climb was called a "zoom." Moving the joystick to either side made the plane turn. A button-trigger set in the joystick fired the machine guns. The pilot's left hand held the throttle, which regulated engine speed. Both feet rested on the rudder bar, used to turn the aircraft by moving the control surfaces on the tail.

Fighter training progressed through four stages. It began with two-seaters, the instructor shouting directions through a rubber hose with a funnel at either end; there was no such thing as air-to-air radio. The cadet then went on to soloing, formation flying and aerobatics—aerial acrobatics or stunt flying.

Aerobatics weren't for showing off or making the pilot look good. Hairpin turns, loops, rolls, and upside-down flying were tricks of the fighter pilot's trade, enabling him to attack or escape as needed. No one was allowed into the war zone without having mastered the *vrille*, French for tailspin, a corkscrew dive that allowed a flyer to drop out of a dangerous situation without losing control of his machine. There were no do-overs with the *vrille*. Either it went well or you spun into the ground.

First World War planes, little better than motorized kites, were dangerous under the best conditions. Smash-ups were normal and everyone expected to lose at least one friend during training. We learn what it was like to fly these crates from *War Birds: The Diary of an Unknown Aviator*, one of the finest accounts of the war in the air. Published anonymously in 1926, it was found among the papers of John McGavock Grider, killed in combat eight years earlier. Grider's diary is filled with passages like these:

> Cush Nathan killed. He was flying [a plane] and the wings came off at five thousand feet. He went into the roof of a three-story house and they dug him out of the basement.

> Bob Griffith is dead. The wings of his [plane] came off at ten thousand feet.

> A horrible thing happened today. We were all out on the tarmac having our pictures taken for posterity when somebody yelled and pointed up. Two [planes] collided right over the airdrome at about three thousand feet. God, it was a horrible sight. . . . They came down in a slow spin with their wings locked together and both of them in flames. Fred Stillman was in one machine and got out alive but badly burned and Doug Ellis was in the other one and was burned to a cinder.

> DeGamo was killed today. Nobody knows how it happened. He was up in a Spad and it was found about five miles from here in a field. . . . It wasn't crashed badly but his neck was broken.

> Montgomery was killed when the pilot fell out of the front seat . . . in a loop.

> Capt. White was landing last week and a tire busted and the wheel gave way and he turned over. The plane caught fire and he was nearly burned to death before we could get him out.

Yet not all crashes were accidental. Sometimes machine guns

jammed in firing position, spewing lead everywhere. One pilot deliberately crashed to keep from shooting down his comrades. Another pilot's engine conked out over a town; it looked as if he'd topple into a crowded street until he brought the nose up just enough to carry him into a field on the outskirts.

There was nothing to do with a crippled plane but pray as you rode it down. Allied and enemy airmen wore no parachutes, and none were issued. As with automobile seat belts today, many pilots foolishly thought parachutes uncomfortable and unmanly. Commanders, moreover, refused to issue parachutes because they thought pilots would lose their nerve, abandoning damaged planes that might otherwise be salvaged. A lot of brave men died needlessly as a result of this attitude.

Despite the dangers, cadets' willingness to take risks grew along with their flying skill. Some forgot that an airplane isn't just a big toy. A cadet broke up a wedding procession outside London by buzzing it at treetop level. He then showed off by looping and rolling between the church spires. Others raised the devil over their base. They'd race their Spads on the ground, then, at the last moment, pull them up in time to run them on the hangar roofs. A cadet chased a machine gun class in and out of its firing pit. He'd dive at them, chase them from the pit, then chase them back in. One cadet in every nineteen was killed in training accidents and harebrained stunts!

Training completed, the new pilots were posted to units behind the front lines. Yank squadrons were stationed mostly in the Toul area south of the old battlefield of Verdun, where a million Frenchmen and Germans had died in 1916.

The typical fighter base, or aerodrome, was simply a cluster of barracks and hangars set amid open fields bordered by forests or apple orchards. Armed guards stood at the fuel tanks and ammunition dumps. Small sheds stood near the headquarters building, their windows covered with heavy black curtains. These belonged to the intelligence sections, which developed aerial photographs and assembled them into large picture-maps of enemy positions. These maps, updated daily and examined inch by inch with powerful magnifying glasses, were used in planning operations. The base had no cement runways; planes simply took off from fields or grass airstrips.

American bases were under the command of Brigadier General William "Billy" Mitchell, chief of air operations, First Army. Mitchell, who'd fought as a private in the Spanish-American War, had several firsts to his credit. He was the first high-ranking United States Army officer to learn to fly, the first to fly over enemy lines, and the first to win the Croix de Guerre.

Billy Mitchell had given much thought to military aviation. The airplane, he believed, was to modern warfare what gunpowder had been to the knights of the Middle Ages. It changed everything. To win a war, a nation must first "own" the sky, otherwise armies and battle fleets were useless. Fighters must clear the sky of enemy planes. Bombers must then fly into the enemy homeland to destroy its vital centers, its railroads, factories, and cities. Total war in the air age meant bringing the battle to the enemy's civilians, the home-front soldiers who supplied the soldiers in the field.

Few Army leaders shared Mitchell's beliefs. The United States Army's brass had little use for airplanes, except as scouts; otherwise they considered them nothing special. Gen-

eral Pershing would never ride in a plane; he once asked
Congress to reduce flyers' pay, claiming that air fighting was
no more dangerous than shouldering a rifle. Black Jack's staff
officers were often old-line cavalrymen who knew nothing
about airplanes and didn't care to learn. One colonel's antics
made Mitchell flush with anger. While inspecting an airfield
on horseback, engine noises frightened his mount. "Stop
those fans!" he shouted at the top of his voice. "Don't you see
they scare my horse?" It took as much effort to educate such
men about airpower as it did to command his flyers in battle.
Let's follow some of them on a routine mission.

A mission for one of Mitchell's squadrons begins before dawn
in the headquarters briefing hall, a large room with rows of
wooden benches. "Ten-shun!" the squadron leader calls as
the base commander, a colonel, enters with his aides: chief
navigator, intelligence officer, weatherman. "At ease, gentlemen," he says, returning their salutes as he steps onto the low
stage in front of the room.

On the stage are large bulletin boards with maps and
photos pinned to them. Some maps have lengths of red ribbon
stretched from Toul to a point in enemy territory. These
indicate the squadron's course. Blue ribbons extend along the
return route. Quickly, precisely, he outlines the day's objective, a long-range patrol behind enemy lines. Pershing's staff
is planning an advance and needs to know what the enemy
is up to.

Pointer in hand, the colonel traces the squadron's course,
identifies fresh German antiaircraft batteries and updates the
enemy order of battle, the fighting units he has in the area.
Although von Richthofen was killed by an Englishman in
April 1918, the Flying Circus is stronger than ever. Its new
commander is Captain Hermann Goering, twenty-five vic-

tories, the future chief of the Luftwaffe. Pilots know they'll have their hands full if they run into the Flying Circus or a sister squadron. A German fighter squadron is called a Jasta, short for *Jagdstaffel*, "hunting squadron." And that's exactly what they are: veteran air fighters stalking their prey. The colonel ends his briefing with a sincere, "Good luck and good hunting." They'll need all the luck they can get.

Pilots bundled in teddy-bear flight suits waddle up to the waiting planes. They're superstitious fellows, even the aces. Everyone has a favorite good luck charm—a religious medal, or rabbit's foot, or coin—to keep him from harm. One wouldn't dream of sitting in a cockpit without a girlfriend's

Fokker fighters of Jasta 11, the Red Baron's Flying Circus. These are biplanes, although Richthofen preferred to go into battle in a blood-red triplane.

silk stocking worn as a scarf. Others make sure of a proper sendoff, should their luck run out. Two of these pilots have had hollow tombstones made for themselves. If they die in German territory, they've asked buddies to fill the stone slabs with TNT and drop them on the enemy; if they crash behind Allied lines, the tombstones will be filled with whiskey to leak on them in their graves.

Each pilot settles into his seat and turns on the motor, which comes to life sputtering and coughing. Just then a sergeant-mechanic grabs a propeller blade and jerks it downward with all his strength. After a couple of false starts, the propeller begins to spin. As its speed increases, other ground crewmen hold onto the plane's wings and tail. This is necessary, because First World War planes have no brakes. A plane has to be held back until the pilot revs the engine to takeoff speed. At his signal, they let go and the plane shoots forward.

Mud spatters up from the field, covering the windshield and the pilot behind it with thick brown gunk. The plane picks up speed, as he opens the throttle all the way and pulls back on the joystick. It shakes and rattles until it leaves the ground with its companions; three or four fighters usually take off from the same field at once. It's an impressive show, and safe—mostly.

The next fifteen minutes are spent in climbing to cruising altitude, ten thousand feet, where the planes take up their formation. A squadron usually sends two flights aloft on any given day. Each flight of seven planes flies in a V-shaped, or wild goose, formation with a leader in front and the back corners high to protect the rear from surprise attack. Larger flights, especially those with two-seater aircraft, form Lufbery Circles.

The planes fly close together and communicate by signals. If the leader wants to turn, he tilts his wing to that side. If he wishes to draw the flight's attention to something, he shakes both wings. If it's the enemy, he shakes his wings and fires his guns. To signal other flights, he fires red, white, or green flares.

The squadron heads eastward, one V behind the other. At first it soars above the French countryside, with its manicured fields and orchards. The sun glistens off the red-tiled roofs of towns along the way. Distant rivers shimmer like silvery serpents. The world, from two miles high, seems so orderly, so peaceful.

That feeling of peacefulness changes to one of stark terror when they approach the front. Even veterans are awed each time they gaze on the landscape below.

It is a vision of hell. The land is barren as far as the eye can see. It's as if an immense steamroller had flattened everything in its path. Only the road pattern, like the strands of a spider's web, is identifiable from aloft.

Moments later the pilots notice long, wormlike wiggles on the ground. The trenches. Then there's row upon row of thin black pencil marks. That's the barbed wire. Beyond is no-man's-land, a moonscape with millions of shell holes.

Sometimes they pass over during a ground bombardment. The sounds of earth seldom carry so high, or penetrate the engines' roar. Yet pilots know when there's a battle. White puffs blossom in clusters, fade, and blossom again. You can't see the shells' effects unless the front has shifted recently and a fresh town comes under fire. Then entire blocks of buildings rise several feet, disintegrate, and settle in a cloud of dust. Low-level flights can actually hear the dull thuds; planes often wobble and bounce from the concussion.

An airman's view of a battlefield, complete with advancing troops, exploding shells, and shell holes. The area is a blasted, poisoned wasteland.

Wise men fly high during poison gas attacks. Witnessing a gas attack from the sky is a terrifying experience, although not as terrifying as being on the receiving end in the trenches. A filthy cloud creeps forward at ground level, in the direction of the wind. If it's chlorine gas, the cloud is pale green; mustard gas clouds are brownish-yellow in color.

The pilots grow restless. They've entered the danger zone; from here on Germans can be expected any moment. To avoid surprises, pilots must constantly turn around in their seats, bank their planes to right and left, look above and around and below every few seconds.

"Beware the Hun in the sun," says an airman's proverb. It's good advice based upon hard experience. Jastas like to cruise at high altitude, with the sun at their backs, almost invisible from below. Many victims never know what's hit them. Out of the sun, a quick burst, and *kaputt*—smashed to bits.

The moment the formations cross no-man's-land, balls of black smoke begin to dot the sky around them. It is anti-aircraft fire, which the pilots call "Archie," after a popular British song. Regardless of whether the shells are Allied or German, they are still Archie. By 1918 both sides had developed quick-firing cannon able to reach the ten-thousand-foot level. Friendly gunners often fire near their own planes to alert them to enemies lurking in the sun or among clouds. Allied Archie bursts with white smoke. German shells burst black, giving off an evil odor that lingers even at high altitude.

The fighters today are getting a workout from German batteries posted along a road to protect truck convoys. Pilots don't worry as long as they can see the shells burst without hearing them. The roar of the engines drowns out distant explosions.

WHAM!

You heard that one, which means you're still alive. But not

for long, because the enemy has your range. To continue
living, you must fool him by changing course. And you must
do it in a split second, without thinking, otherwise the next
shots will have you. With motor racing, joystick pulled back
as far as it will go, you zoom almost straight up. Your ears
pop, and your stomach seems to be slipping into your boots,
but that's better than flying into the black puffs that open
where you would have been in another second.

One pilot isn't fast enough, and his plane vanishes in a
blinding flash. His comrades feel the heat as they fly through
the flaming wreckage. Another man feels his plane shudder
but, since nothing else happens, remains in formation. After
the mission, his mechanic will find a dud, an unexploded shell,
wedged in the engine compartment. All he can do is swallow
hard and rub his rabbit's foot.

This time the flight leader decides to give the enemy gunners a taste of their own medicine. While the other formation
continues on course, he fires a burst and points his plane's nose
downward. The entire flight lines up behind him and dives
with engines screaming. Lieutenant Hamilton Coolidge later
described such an attack; it is called "strafing," from the
German word for punishment.

How my old heart just hammered with excitement as I
dove down beside that road, not fifty feet high, and recognized those Boche helmets! In a twinkling I was past them,
gained a little height to turn in safety, and came diving
down upon them from the rear. . . . The fiery bullets flew
streaming out of the two guns. Little glimpses was all I
could catch before I was by. Another turn and down the
line again. I had a vague confused picture of streaming fire,
of rearing horses, falling men, running men, general mess.
Turn again and back upon them. This time I clearly saw
two men heel off the seat of a wagon, and then more awful

mess. A fourth time I turned and came back. . . . . Horses rearing, falling men; wagons crosswise in the road; men again dashing for the gutter. . . . I found myself trembling with excitement and overawed at being a cold-blooded murderer, but a sense of keen satisfaction came too. It was only the sort of thing our poor Doughboys had suffered so often.

Climbing back to altitude, the flight continues its patrol. Ten minutes later the pilot at the upper left corner of the formation cuts loose with his machine guns and breaks away. His comrades, glancing over their shoulders, discover the reason for his excitement. There, at ten o'clock, diving out of the sun, comes a swarm of brightly painted airplanes with black crosses on their wings. It is Jasta 11, the Flying Circus.

The Yanks break formation for a dogfight, a free-for-all at ten thousand feet. Sometimes dogfights spread over a wide area, drawing in other squadrons until over a hundred planes are battling on each side. The troops in the trenches have grandstand seats; for once they're not the center of attraction and mean to enjoy the show. Whenever an enemy hurtles earthward, trailing a banner of flames, they cheer as though the home team has scored; an Allied loss draws loud boos.

The sky is alive with fighters zooming, diving, banking, and shooting. Pilots, misjudging their turns, crash head-on or pancake, one plane dropping on top of the other, destroying both. From the corner of his eye a pilot notices the fabric peel off his tail during a tight turn. Planes crumple during power dives for no apparent reason.

Despite the seeming confusion, flyers follow certain basic tactics. It is best to begin by diving at the enemy out of the sun, except when attacking a two-seater with a rear gunner, who'll give you a faceful of lead. In that case, you must come at him from below, riddling his underside. Another favored position is behind the enemy's tail. Even if there is a rear gunner, he can't get at you without blasting away his own plane's tail.

The advantage, however, isn't always the attacker's. The intended victim can usually turn the tables if he's clever enough and fast. When attacked by a diving enemy, the underdog must turn and climb toward him, meeting him face to face. The planes close with each other at terrific speed, machine guns blazing. On they come, until one explodes or is shot down. If not, one has to turn chicken, swerve out of the way to avoid a collision. This maneuver takes steady nerves on the part of both flyers and is often used as a test of courage and skill.

An attack from behind may be met with an Immelmann Turn, named for the German ace Max Immelmann. The idea is to zoom almost straight up, make a half-turn, and come down behind your pursuer. Pilots often wind up chasing each other in circles this way—until one decides he's had enough and dives for safety.

But whatever the tactic, there is one basic rule in air fighting: Do anything to get the enemy before he gets you. This means that the pilot and not his machine is the true target. Fighter pilots are taught to aim high, killing their man quickly with bullets to the head and chest. That's why they use tracers; every eighth bullet is filled with a chemical that traces a white or colored line, allowing the pilot to see where his bullets are hitting and correct his aim. It isn't enough to see an enemy hit and go down. The pilot must follow him down to make sure he crashes. It's nasty work, for he's usually close enough to see his victim slumped over the controls of the spinning aircraft.

Defenseless enemies are fair game. Sometimes an opponent

suddenly stops shooting. A closer look reveals him hammering away at one of his machine guns; a bullet has jammed in the firing chamber and must be knocked loose with a hammer kept for the purpose.

Georges Guynemer let these unfortunates escape with a wave of his hand. Most airmen, however, Allied as well as German, shot them down. The American ace Douglas Campbell was attacking a two-seater camera plane when he noticed that the machine gunner had used up his ammunition. "So I just had to get up behind him and shoot him down—cold—it made me sort of sick." Yet the plane couldn't be allowed to escape with valuable pictures, although Campbell felt sorry for its crew.

The flyer's greatest fear wasn't of dying, but of dying in a certain way. To be shot cleanly or crash from ten thousand feet was painless; most men became unconscious long before they hit the ground. But to burn in a gasoline fire, that was the most horrible death pilots could imagine. Their names for gasoline told of their fears: Orange Death, The Hell-brew, Witches' Water, Infernal Liquid. Those fears gave them recurring nightmares or kept them awake, shivering in the long hours before dawn.

It only took a leaky fuel line or a bullet in the gas tank to turn nightmare into reality. If the pilot was lucky, his plane exploded, ending his agony. If he was unlucky, his plane spun earthward wrapped in smoke and flame.

Sooner or later most airmen had a close look inside the cockpit of a burning plane. The crew, their hair and clothing on fire, writhed in pain, slowly broiling to a crisp. Sometimes they stood up to flail their arms and shout curses; others shot themselves with revolvers or leaped out, arms outstretched, as if to fly. Very few had the skill and, what is more, the luck to keep control of a burning plane. Going into a stall could smother the flames with a back draft. Finding a river to land in before the flames reached them also worked. One American crawled out on the wing of his Spad and reached into the flaming cockpit to handle the joystick. Though badly burned, he guided the craft into a clump of bushes, jumping clear at the last instant. He survived, recovered, and rejoined his unit.

Its patrol finished, our squadron turns for home. As they recross the Allied lines, some pilots shut off their engines and glide the rest of the way. It's a great feeling, coming in without power. Suddenly all is silent, save for the rushing of the wind and the moaning of the wires in the rigging. Men are so exhausted by now that the gentle rocking lulls a few to sleep. (Lieutenant Jeffers of the 94th Squadron awoke ten feet above his airstrip, in time to crash-land safely.) Others land normally. Lacking brakes, they switch their engines on and off, slowing down until ground crews can grab their wings and bring them to a full stop.

Yet the battle isn't over. One can go through many dogfights without a scratch and still be badly wounded. Like the shell-shocked Doughboys, the airmen carried painful wounds inside themselves. These young fliers had seen too many awful things not to be shaken by their experiences. Many cracked up, suffered nervous breakdowns after a few weeks in combat. They had trouble sleeping, and when sleep finally did come it was haunted by the ghosts of victims and friends. Each brush with death was endured several times: first in reality, then in recurring nightmares.

Then there was the knowledge that luck would surely desert them one day. It was only a question of the odds catching up. Every squadron lost over half its pilots within a few weeks—killed, captured, wounded, crippled. In time, if you kept flying, your number would come up, even if you were a super-ace.

John McGavock Grider described his feelings in a long passage in his diary. More than sixty years later, it still has the power to move us with its sadness.

. . . we've lost a lot of good men. It's only a question of time until we all get it. I'm all shot to pieces. I only hope I can stick it. I don't want to quit. My nerves are all gone and I can't stop. I've lived beyond my time already. . . . Here I am, twenty-four years old, I look forty and feel ninety. I've lost all interest in life beyond the next patrol. No one Hun will ever get me and I'll never fall into a trap, but sooner or later I'll be forced to fight against odds that are too long or perhaps a stray shot from the ground will be lucky and I will have gone in vain. Or my motor will cut out when we are trench strafing or a wing will pull off in a dive. . . . It gives me a dizzy feeling every time I hear of the men that are gone. And they have gone so fast I can't keep track of them; every time two pilots meet it is only to swap news of who's killed. When a person takes sick, lingers in bed a few days, dies and is buried on the third day, it all seems regular and they pass on into the great beyond in an orderly manner and you accept their departure as an accomplished fact. But when you lunch with a man, talk to him, see him go out and get in his plane in the prime of his youth and the next day someone tells you that he is dead—it just doesn't sink in and you can't believe it. And the oftener it happens the harder it is to believe. I've lost over a hundred friends, so they tell me . . . but to me they aren't dead yet. They are just around the corner, I think, and I'm still expecting to run into them any time. I dream about them at night when I do sleep a little.

Grider was shot down in flames a few days after writing these lines.

Those who thought the fly-boys had it too easy had a lot to learn.

Different squadrons became famous for different reasons. Major Harry Brown's 96th Squadron earned its nickname of First Bewilderment Group. In July 1918, Brown, who had little combat experience, led a flight of two-seater Breguet bombers on a raid behind enemy lines in France. The weather report, which called for thickening clouds as the day wore on, should have made him cautious. Brown ignored the weatherman's advice and took off with six planes.

The weather turned foul almost immediately. Clouds hid the ground, blotting out any landmarks. With their fuel running low, the clouds parted just enough to allow the planes to drop through and head for some clearings near a wide river. No one recognized the river, nor was anything like it on their maps of the front-line areas.

As the aircraft bounced to a stop, civilians came running across the clearings to meet them.

"Where are we?" a pilot asked in French.

Nobody answered.

Someone else, suspicious by now, repeated the question in broken German: "*Wo bist . . . ?*"

This time the civilians answered. The river they'd seen was the Rhine; they had landed deep inside Germany.

A few days later a lone Albatros darted over an American aerodrome and dropped a message for Billy Mitchell. It said, "We thank you for the fine airplanes and equipment which you have sent us, but what shall we do with the major?" Mitchell didn't reply, as Major Brown was safer for the

moment in an enemy prison camp than he'd have been at
First Army headquarters.

The 96th's sister squadron would have done anything to
bring back *its* major. When the Lafayette Escadrille went out
of existence, its members joined American outfits. Raoul
Lufbery, the Lafayette's leading ace, became a major and
took command of the 94th Squadron. The 94th's insignia
was an American flag shaped like an Uncle Sam stovepipe
hat with a red ring around it. This symbol meant that Uncle
Sam had tossed his hat into the ring, joining the air war over
Europe.

The youngsters of the Hat-in-the-Ring Squadron came to
love "Luf." This battle-toughened veteran was like a mamma
lion caring for her cubs. He let them know, without ever
saying it in words, that their lives were precious to him. He'd
never allow a newcomer to go into battle without first taking
him on trial runs over enemy territory. Lufbery watched his
every move, covering his tail in case the Germans put in an

*Major Raoul Lufbery, right, talks with a friend in April, 1918.
Notice the Hat-in-the-Ring emblem on the fuselage of the Spad
behind them.*

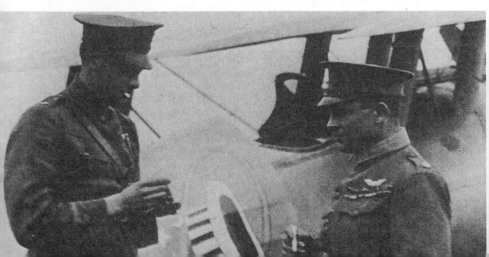

appearance. After the flight, he'd point out his errors and explain how to correct them.

On the morning of May 19, 1918, an alert came that a German camera plane had crossed the lines and was heading for the 94th's aerodrome. Hearing the alarm, Lufbery leaped on a motorcycle and raced for the hangars. His own machine was with the mechanics, so seeing another parked nearby, he asked if it was gassed and armed. It was, and he took off a moment later.

By now hundreds of men had gathered on the field, eager to see the great Lufbery in action. What they saw brought tears to their eyes.

Lufbery climbed above the German, then dived, firing short bursts as he sped by. Then, apparently, his guns jammed. Regaining altitude, he circled above the German until he had cleared the jam and closed in for the kill. As he bore in on the German's tail, his plane suddenly burst into flame. The enemy gunner, shooting wildly, had put a stream of tracers into his gas tank.

The men below watched horrified as the ball of fire careened earthward. Seconds later, they saw Lufbery stand in the cockpit and leap to certain death rather than endure the torture of roasting alive.

His comrades found him a half-hour later. Loving hands had already moved the body to a nearby town hall. There farmers covered the charred remains with a mound of flowers from their gardens.

Next day Raoul Lufbery was laid to rest in a hospital graveyard with full military honors. The coffin was being lowered into the earth when the droning of motors came on the breeze. The sound grew louder until the Hat-in-the-Ring came overhead in a V of Vs, like a huge spearhead without a shaft. Approaching the gravesite at treetop level, the pilots turned off their engines, gliding over in silent tribute. As each plane passed, its pilot dropped a bouquet of wildflowers onto the raw earth.

The first V was led by Captain Eddie Rickenbacker, soon to become America's leading ace with twenty-six official victories. Born in 1890 in Columbus, Ohio, Eddie quit school at twelve to support his widowed mother. Love for his mother was to inspire him all his life; indeed, it saved his life. When she heard that he wanted to fly in combat, she wrote him to "fly slow and stay close to the ground." He claimed the thought of her grief at his death gave him the strength to fight his way out of at least one tight spot.

Captain Edward Vernon Rickenbacker, commander of the Hat-in-the-Ring Squadron, sits in the cockpit of his Spad, behind its two forward-firing machine guns.

Eddie's earliest jobs had nothing to do with aviation. He began as an errand boy in a factory for $3.50 a week, all of which he gave to his mother. In his teens he became interested in machinery and went to work for a small-time automobile manufacturer. One thing led to another, and before long he took up auto racing. By 1917 he was earning $40,000 a year as one of the world's top racing drivers.

Although he could have spent the war safely as a general's chauffeur, he wanted to become a pilot. "Rick," as everyone called him, hated the cruelty and waste of war. Yet the idea of sky-fighting fascinated him as a sportsman. A born competitor, he was eager to match his skill against Germany's aviators for the highest stakes of all: their lives.

Rick volunteered for flight training and stuck with it despite the difficulties. Not that he feared heights or doubted his ability to control a plane. Airsickness was his problem. He couldn't bounce about in the air currents without his stomach churning. It took every ounce of willpower to keep from vomiting until he finally won the battle with himself.

After passing his course, he was posted to the Hat-in-the-Ring. As usual, Lufbery took Rickenbacker and another newcomer, Douglas Campbell, on their first expedition over the lines. That patrol taught them some life-saving lessons. Everything seemed easy as falling off a log. Except for some badly aimed Archie, the Germans gave them a free ride.

Rickenbacker and Campbell felt pretty good when they landed. Surely, they boasted, the dangers of combat flying were overrated. German pilots must be cowards, otherwise they would have come up after them.

Lufbery broke into the conversation and, chuckling to himself, asked if they'd seen any planes during the flight. When they said none, he reeled off what *he*'d seen: fifteen aircraft, Allied and enemy, fighters and camera planes. Had the enemy taken the trouble, he could have knocked them to pieces before they knew what hit them. Luf had deliberately embarrassed them in public to take out some of their arrogance. It worked. From then on both men began to score against the enemy.

Rickenbacker, however, was in a class by himself. The skills that made him a successful racing driver now served him in the air. Racing had gotten him used to danger, to dizzying speeds, to judging distances and making split-second decisions; watching an opponent's actions and predicting his next moves came naturally to him.

Rickenbacher knew, above all, the value of caution. In the air, as on the speedway, his motto was: "Never take an unnecessary risk." He did everything humanly possible to load the odds in his favor. Every morning without fail he checked his engines personally; he knew by the sound if anything was wrong. He even sorted through his machine gun bullets for misshapen shells that might jam a gun.

When Lufbery's replacement was shot down several weeks later, Billy Mitchell made Rick squadron commander. Other officers had served longer and were better educated than Rickenbacker, the school dropout. But Mitchell passed them over, for he saw in Rickenbacker the makings of a great combat leader. He never regretted his decision.

Responsibility for the lives of others turned Rickenbacker into the best squadron commander in the Air Service; indeed, it is difficult to think of another airman in either world war who matched him as an all-around leader. "Just promoted to command the 94th Squadron," he wrote in his diary. "I must work harder than I did before."

Everyone must work harder. On the day of his promotion

he called a squadron meeting to lay down the law. It was a hard law, but fair. Rickenbacker demanded the best from his men, as he demanded it from himself, all the time. He wouldn't settle for less, and God help the fellow who thought otherwise. Stupidity he could understand and forgive, maybe; carelessness and laziness were unpardonable sins.

Rickenbacker was always dressed and out of his quarters before sunup, inspecting the base as if it were the family farm. Waste was a crime in his book. Parts that could be salvaged had to be repaired and used again. If a mechanic didn't know how to save a part, he'd show him.

But most of all Rickenbacker hated to waste human life. Part of his duty as squadron commander was to write letters to the families of men killed in action. He took an oath that he'd write as few of these letters as possible. We can hear the spirit of Raoul Lufbery speaking through him in this diary notation: "I should never ask any pilot under me to go on a mission that I myself would not undertake. . . . I would accompany the new pilots and watch their errors and help them to feel more confidence by sharing their dangers."

Rickenbacker ran the Hat-in-the-Ring like an aerial football team with himself as head coach. He drummed it into his pilots' heads that although they might be aces they were part of a team. If a man couldn't be a teamplayer, he was useless; indeed, dangerous; for he might endanger others' lives.

Rickenbacker began the buddy system, whereby two pilots were specially assigned to look after each other. The squadron mess hall doubled as a schoolroom, complete with charts, chalkboard, and lectures. Battles and tactics were always discussed during meals with an eye to improvement. Strict as he was, the men realized that Rick cared deeply about them. His quick smile and reassuring words convinced them that he was more than a commander. He was a friend.

Rickenbacker set an example with his own exploits. On the morning of September 15, 1918, the day after taking command, he downed two Fokkers before breakfast. During the next two weeks he destroyed another dozen planes of various types. By the end of October he'd logged his twenty-sixth kill, plus about a dozen unconfirmed enemy planes that fell on the other side of the lines, making him America's official Ace of Aces.

Yet the title Ace of Aces didn't make him happy. He had the superstitious fear that it was jinxed, a death sentence rather than something to cheer about. All of its previous holders had been killed, including Lufbery. He also knew the odds, and that his luck, too, was bound to change. It was this very fear that made him redouble his caution and sharpen his fighting skills, becoming a better pilot than ever.

His Hat-in-the-Ring became America's answer to the Flying Circus. When the war ended, it led all other Air Service squadrons with sixty-nine official victories, nearly half of which belonged to its commander.

Rickenbacker returned home to a hero's welcome and the Medal of Honor, the nation's highest award for gallantry. In the years that followed he became an automobile manufacturer and president of Eastern Airlines. He served during the Second World War as an adviser to the United States Air Force. While on an inspection tour of air bases in the Pacific, his plane crash-landed at sea. The survivors were rescued after twenty-three days adrift in shark-infested waters. He died in 1973 in his eighty-second year.

The Medal of Honor was awarded to only one other First World War pilot, a youngster different from Rickenbacker in every way save courage and fighting skill. His name was Frank Luke. Rickenbacker knew him, liked him, admired him. Luke, he said flatly, was "the greatest fighting pilot of the war"—no small compliment, coming from our Ace of Aces.

In 1918 Luke was a lanky blond twenty-one year old from Arizona. Difficult to get along with, he either kept to himself in bashful silence or praised himself as God's gift to aviation. As a boy he'd roamed the mountains of his home state on foot, making a living as a copper miner. Mining was heavy, dirty work and it toughened him; his fellow miners, tough guys all, taught him to use his fists.

When America went to war, Luke joined the Signal Corps and applied for flight training. He was a natural aviator. Nothing seemed to faze him. It was as if his mind were in tune with his plane's engine, his muscles and nerves connected to its control surfaces. He flew beautifully, gracefully, always in control.

Luke completed flight training two weeks ahead of his class and was commissioned a second lieutenant assigned to the 27th Squadron near Château-Thierry. No teamplayer, he was a wild mustang hellbent on doing things his own way. At first his squadronmates laughed, calling him a braggart, all talk and no action. Then, within seventeen days, from September 12 to 29, he scored twenty-one victories, a record unmatched in any air force during the First World War.

What made Luke so special wasn't merely the number of his victories, but the types of aircraft destroyed. With the exception of three enemy planes, all his victories were over observation balloons. For Frank Luke was leader of a select group of pilots: the balloon-busters.

These huge gas-filled bags must have looked like easy targets to outsiders. They just hung there, at perhaps a thousand feet, swaying at the ends of steel cables tethered to the ground. Both sides used them as observation posts to report troop movements and direct artillery fire by telephone. Dur-

Lieutenant Frank Luke of the 27th Squadron was America's ace balloon-buster. He was shot down before he could be court-martialed for being absent without leave or receive the Medal of Honor he also deserved.

ing bombardments, observers told the gunners where their shells were falling and how to adjust their aim to get right on target.

Attacking balloons, which the Germans called *Drachen* (dragons) was the specialty of daredevils who seldom survived more than a few missions. The attacker had to run a gauntlet of defenses in order to come within striking distance. Relays of fighters orbited overhead, waiting to pounce on the unwary. Antiaircraft batteries and machine gun companies waited on the ground, their weapons zeroed in on the approaches to the balloon. These antiaircraft batteries didn't fire ordinary Archie, but "flaming onions," shells filled with white phosphorous, a chemical that bursts into flame on contact with air, covering a wide area.

Any flyer who came through this curtain of fire could easily destroy the balloon with tracers. The gas began to burn the moment the bullets struck the bag, exploding it within fifteen seconds. The two-man crew had to jump or fry. Unlike pilots, balloonists had parachutes, so that most survived. Some balloonists made over five hundred emergency jumps during the war.

The Germans often set out decoy balloons to trap the inexperienced. An Allied flyer, seeing an "unguarded" balloon, would swoop down with machine guns chattering. Coming closer, he might notice that there was nobody in the passenger basket suspended below the bag. We'll never know what he saw or how he felt; he never survived. The basket contained a ton of amatol, a super-powerful explosive, detonated from the ground when he drew near.

Luke was the world's champion balloon-buster. He'd set off each morning with his only friend, Lieutenant Joseph Wehner, a big quiet man from Boston. When they found a target, Wehner would climb above it to draw away the fighter cover while Luke dove for the kill. Once an attack began, Luke kept going no matter what came at him from the ground. One pass, a quick burst, and another *Drachen* exploded. Each balloon cost the kaiser nearly as much as a whole squadron of fighters.

Luke became so expert at balloon-busting that he could call his shots in advance. During a visit to the Hat-in-the-Ring, he noticed two *Drachen* in the distance. "Keep your eyes on these two balloons," he told Rickenbacker. "You will see that first one go down in flames exactly at 7:15 and the other will do likewise at 7:19." He kept his word, both balloons catching fire on schedule.

One day Luke and his partner sighted two balloons. As

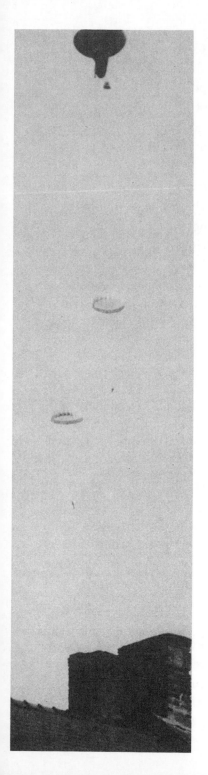

Balloon-busting. Two men have just parachuted out of the passenger basket hanging below the balloon in the left hand picture; moments later, the balloon plummets to earth in flames.

usual, Wehner took up a defensive position while Luke dove to the attack. Luke had destroyed both balloons when he saw six Fokkers moving to block his way back to Allied lines. Glancing over his shoulder, he saw three more Fokkers speeding to get on his tail.

Just when he thought he was a goner, Wehner dove into their path, leveled off, and charged them head-on. The three Germans opened fire at once, turning the Spad into a ball of flame. Wehner had deliberately sacrificed himself to save his friend.

Luke, furious and bent on revenge, now gave a display of combat flying unmatched in both world wars. Instead of escaping in the few seconds Wehner had bought him with his life, he attacked the three Fokkers. They were no match for him.

The Arizonan got on the tail of one Fokker, ignoring the others, who were on *his* tail. Tracers flashed by his head. His tail began to resemble Swiss cheese. Yet he clung to his prey, firing short, well-aimed bursts until he spun out of control. He then pulled back the joystick and zoomed straight up. The Spad's engine screamed, its wings shivered, as he looped behind the second Fokker, blowing him to bits with one burst. The third Fokker turned tail and raced for home.

But Luke wasn't finished. He dodged the six other Fokkers and, for good measure, downed a two-seater camera plane while crossing the lines. In under twenty minutes, he'd destroyed five enemy aircraft against overwhelming odds— a deed unmatched in warfare.

"Has Wehner come back?" he asked as soon as he landed, already knowing the answer. Wehner's death made him even more of a loner. He became defiant, breaking the rules when- ever he pleased. He went AWOL—Absent Without Leave— after one mission, landing at another field to spend the night with a French escadrille. That was the last straw. Ace or not, his commander decided to court-martial him and recommend him for the Medal of Honor at the same time. He deserved both.

Next morning, September 29, 1918, Luke saw three *Drachen* while returning to the 27th's field. Before attacking, he dropped a message to American troops telling them to keep their eyes on the balloons. Two minutes later, a red glow in the sky indicated that he'd scored. He had already set the second balloon ablaze when two Fokkers pounced on him from above.

This time there was no escape. Wounded, his plane trailing a plume of smoke, he came in low over the village of Murvaux. German troops were in the streets, firing at him with rifles and machine guns. Luke kept shooting at them until his Spad slammed into the local cemetery.

Groggy from loss of blood, he whipped out his pistol and leaned against the wreck, waiting for the soldiers to find him. The Germans, who admired his courage, wanted to take him alive. They demanded that he surrender, but when he fired at them they shot him dead.

Lieutenant Mangels, the local German commander, took his flyer's badge as a souvenir. Luke, he said, "was a man of dazzling courage, one of the bravest we fought in the war." On this, at least, his friends and enemies could agree. Arizona's Luke Air Force Base is dedicated to the memory of America's ace balloon-buster.

The American Air Service destroyed a total of 781 enemy planes and 73 balloons during the First World War. But more important than mere numbers, Rickenbacker, Luke, Lufbery, and the others began a tradition of excellence that continues to this day in the United States Air Force.

SEVEN

Breakthrough to Victory

On a rainy summer afternoon late in August 1918, Ferdinand Foch leaned over the map table in his headquarters at Bombon southeast of Paris. Foch, recently promoted to field marshal, had been poring over maps of the Western Front for days. The more closely he examined the maps, the more convinced he became that a bold move would break the back of the German armies, ending the war by winter.

The Allied supreme commander knew that the enemy was growing weaker. He could read it in the battle reports. The failure of Ludendorff's spring offensive had cost nearly a half-million casualties, killed and wounded, with nothing to show for the effort. Morale, the willpower soldiers need to keep fighting despite setbacks, was crumbling. The German troops had expected to drive the British into the English Channel and punch through to Paris. But Tommies and poilus, stiffened by Doughboys, had held firm, forcing them back. The Germans became so gloomy that one soldier wrote that you could cut it with a bayonet. The German home front, suffering from years of privation due to the blockade, began to lose hope.

A German war prisoner at a seaport where a troop convoy had anchored stopped work for a moment to stare at the Doughboys marching down the gangplanks. He turned to an American military policeman and asked how many were landing that day. When he heard forty or fifty thousand, the German's eyes filled with tears and he said, *"Mein Gott in Himmel!"*—"My God in Heaven!" He knew instantly that the war was lost. Germany's cause was hopeless, and the sooner she made peace the better for everyone.

Foch meant to have peace soon on the Allies' terms. He knew the real troop arrival figures, and they were amazing. In March, when Ludendorff's offensive began, seventy-five thousand Yanks arrived in France. By June, when the Marines stormed Belleau Wood, they were coming at the rate of two hundred thousand a month. By August, Foch noted that a million and a half Americans had entered the trenches, were preparing to enter them, or were manning the lines of communication in the rear. That number would climb to two million within a few weeks. At last the Allies had both the initiative and the numerical superiority. Foch intended to use them both.

To understand his plan, let's imagine the Western Front as an immense hook-shaped scythe with its inner, or cutting, edge opening toward the enemy. The Belgian army, tiny and tough, was the blade's point; King Albert of Belgium led his troops in person. The Allied main force, the British under Field Marshal Sir Douglas Haig and the French under Field Marshal Philippe Pétain, formed the blade's central arc. Black Jack Pershing's First Army, soon to be joined by the Second

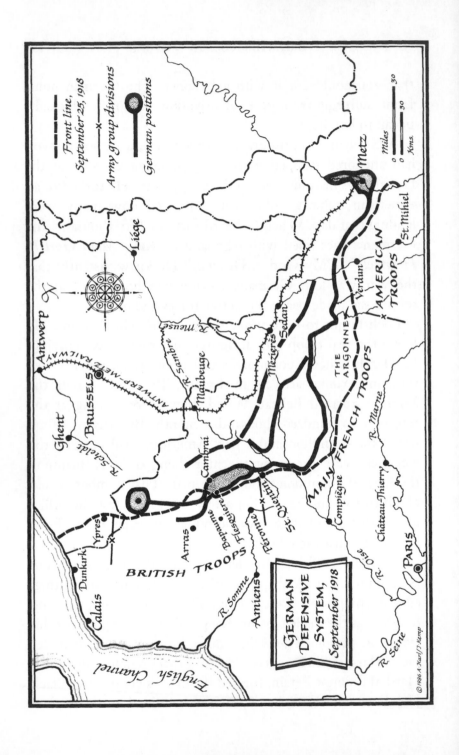

GERMAN DEFENSIVE SYSTEM, September 1918

Army, was the straight part of the blade near the handle.

Foch planned to swing the scythe from south to north; the Americans would strike first, followed by each of the Allies in turn. The objective was not to fight the enemy along the entire five hundred miles of front, but to seize certain key points. The Americans and French were to go for Méziers and Sedan, cities taken by Germany during the war of 1870. The British were to thrust eastward toward Cambrai and Lille, in the general direction of Maubeuge, Belgium. The Belgians would take the high ground at Ypres Ridge, over-looking the right wing of the German front.

The cities, however, were the keys to victory. Each was a major link along the Antwerp-Metz railway, which ran behind the entire length of the German front. Here was the enemy's jugular vein, the main supply line for his armies in the West and his escape route back to Germany. Cut this line anywhere, and the German front collapsed.

Foch expected stiff resistance. Before his scythe reached the jugular, it had to slice through the strongest defense system ever built. The Germans had spent four years putting a barrier between the Allies and their precious railroad. This barrier was the dread Hindenburg Line, named for Field Marshal Paul von Hindenburg, Ludendorff's chief and Chief of the German Imperial General Staff.

The Hindenburg Line was really three sets of defensive positions, one behind the other, stretching eastward to a depth of fifteen to twenty miles. These positions were thickets of camouflaged machine gun nests supported by underground forts with concrete roofs fifteen feet thick and surrounded by belts of barbed wire. Only a direct hit with the heaviest shells could crack these fortifications. Moreover, woods and hills had been leveled to give German gunners

Field Marshal Paul von Hindenburg was chief of the German Imperial General Staff, next to the Kaiser the supreme commander of the army.

clear fields of fire. Every village and town in the defensive zone had been emptied of civilians and turned into a strongpoint; towns that couldn't be used for defense were destroyed. Without the numerical superiority the Americans gave him, Foch wouldn't have dreamed of breaking through this death zone. Even so, breaking the Hindenburg Line wasn't going to be a picnic.

Before launching the campaign, Allied commanders had to decide what to do about the St.-Mihiel salient. Since 1914 St.-Mihiel, a town ten miles south of Verdun on the Meuse River, had been the tip of an annoying bulge in the Allied line. Foch, anxious to begin the big push, didn't think the salient was worth bothering about; it could be sealed off by a few divisions to prevent an enemy breakout.

Black Jack wasn't so sure. The Germans, he said, must be driven from St.-Mihiel to protect the Allied right wing once the offensive began. Foch not only disagreed with him, but demanded that the First Army be broken up and placed under French and British command. Pershing's temper flared when he heard this; there was no way he'd allow an American army to be taken from American control.

Both men stood toe to toe, eye to eye, shouting. Officers, fearing they'd use their fists, managed to calm them down. Foch finally agreed to Pershing's idea, but on two conditions: that the Yanks pinch off the salient and that it be done in time for them to join the main battle.

Foch had given the Americans a difficult, perhaps an impossible, task. Pershing had to lead a huge army in a major battle. He had to win that battle and then, within ten days, shift the army northward some fifty miles over a network of narrow, unpaved country roads. And, of course, the movement would have to be at night in complete secrecy. Black Jack had no choice but to accept the Frenchman's challenge and get to work.

St.-Mihiel was to be the biggest battle in American history up to that time. Compared to St.-Mihiel, the entire American Revolution was a skirmish. With the force at his command— troops, tanks, artillery, planes—Pershing could have wiped out the combined Union and Confederate armies during the Civil War in a few hours.

Everything about St.-Mihiel had to be thought of, planned for, in advance. A half-million Yanks and a hundred thousand poilus had to be moved according to precise timetables to avoid traffic jams. Much of the planning for the First Army was done by Lieutenant Colonel George C. Marshall. A tall, serious-looking man of thirty-seven, Marshall was a human dynamo and a computer rolled into one. No assignment was too difficult for him. Brother officers trusted him as a person who knew what he was doing and always did it well. One day he'd be Army Chief of Staff and Secretary of State; his

Lieutenant.Colonel George C. Marshall was one of the masterminds behind the planning of the Meuse–Argonne offensive.

Marshall Plan was largely responsible for rebuilding Europe after the Second World War.

Marshall saw to it that G-2, the Military Intelligence Service, kept field commanders up-to-date on enemy strength and positions. Printing presses ran overtime in guarded sheds, turning out the hundred thousand maps the assault troops would need. He saw to it that thirty-five hospital trains stood at sidings behind the front. Fifty thousand tons of artillery shells rolled toward the front in caissons, two-wheeled ammunition wagons drawn by horses.

The shells would be fired from three thousand cannon of all sizes, ranging from light field artillery to the 155-millimeter "Long Toms" based ten miles behind the front. There was also a battery of naval guns, mammoths of the type used on battleships to throw one-ton shells twenty miles.

Tanks rattled and snorted up to their jump-off positions. These weapons, painted in weird green, red, and brown patterns, were new to war. A British invention, tanks were designed to clear paths through barbed wire and wipe out machine gun nests ahead of advancing infantry. *Tank* was the codeword used to keep the weapon secret until its first use in 1917.

First World War tanks were either "male" or "female." Male, or heavy tanks, carried machine guns and a small cannon; female tanks had only machine guns. Neither was very comfortable. They bounced along on tractor treads, shaking their crews until their heads reeled. And they were hot, because of the lack of insulation near the engine. With luck, a crew might bake in one of these 140 degree ovens for an hour without fainting.

The tanks at St.-Mihiel were all borrowed from the French, although half had American crews. Their commander was

American tanks going into action during the Meuse–Argonne offensive. Small, lightly armed, and having thin armor plate, these tanks were the forerunners of the armored divisions of the Second World War.

Major George S. Patton, Jr. During the next war, *General* Patton, "Old Blood and Guts," as his men called him, would lead our armored spearheads into the heart of Nazi Germany.

Early in the morning of September 12, 1918, assault troops filed into the forward trenches. Eight American divisions—1st, 2nd, 5th, 15th, 26th, 42nd, 89th, 90th—plus five French divisions half their size were to lead the attack. Other units, including the Marine Brigade, were in reserve to be used as needed.

At exactly 1:00 A.M. the American artillery roared in unison, creating a false dawn with their gunflashes. The waiting troops cupped their hands over their ears against the shock waves. Men filing past the guns felt the hot breath on their faces.

The Germans, who'd been expecting an attack, had begun to withdraw from the salient to stronger positions near the city of Metz. The bombardment caught them off balance, just as they were pulling out. Their artillery replied weakly; their infantry began to flee in panic.

At 5:00 A.M. the barrage lifted. Tanks emerged from the predawn haze, clanging and toppling toward the barbed-wire entanglements. Sergeants blew their whistles. Cries of "Let's go!" rippled along the American front. Then, burdened with packs and shovels and guns, the Doughboys went over the top.

They were moving forward nicely when the sun began to burn off the haze. As visibility improved, sirens wailed in scores of Allied aerodromes. Planes, already fueled and armed, took off in swarms. Forming Vs, they soared over the advancing infantry. Soldiers looked up, shielding their eyes against the sun, and cheered.

Billy Mitchell had massed fifteen hundred planes, the

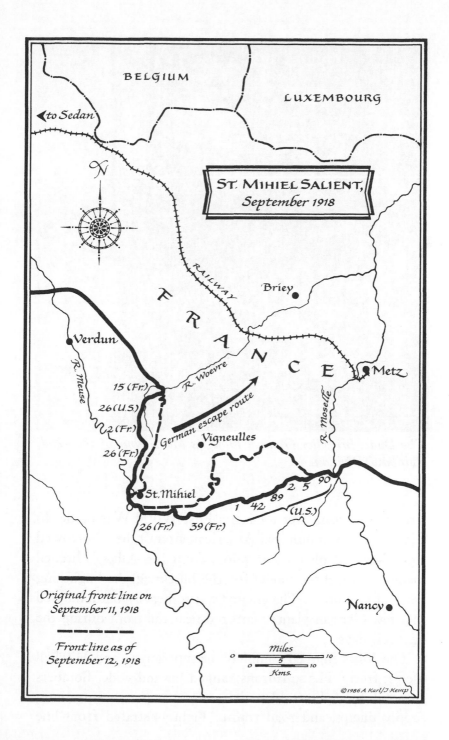

St. Mihiel Salient,
September 1918

BELGIUM

LUXEMBOURG

to Sedan

N

FRANCE

RAILWAY

Briey

Verdun

R. Woevre

R. Meuse

Metz

15 (Fr.)

26 (U.S.)

2 (Fr.)

German escape route

Vigneulles

R. Moselle

26 (Fr.)

St. Mihiel

2, 5, 90

1 42 89 (U.S.)

26 (Fr.)   39 (Fr.)

Nancy

Original front line on
September 11, 1918

Front line as of
September 12, 1918

Miles
0   5   10
0   5   10
Kms.

©1986 A. Karl/J. Kemp

The Dude. Brigadier General Douglas MacArthur of the 42nd, Rainbow, Division.

largest air armada ever used in a First World War battle. In addition to seven hundred American aircraft, he'd borrowed eight hundred planes and pilots from the Allies. Mitchell made St.-Mihiel the model for the blitzkrieg, the "lightning war" of the future. The enemy was so heavily outnumbered that few German planes ventured near the front during the next few days.

The Allies enjoyed complete air superiority, and Mitchell used it freely. His squadrons ranged far and wide. Bombers escorted by fighters blasted enemy troop concentrations, supply dumps, and road traffic. Fighters strafed front-line trenches as well as airfields behind the lines. Retreat became a rout, as Americans actually began running after the fleeing Germans.

Among those who ran fastest were the men of the 42nd Infantry Division, nicknamed the "Rainbow," because it had units from half the states in the Union. Some Rainbow outfits and commanders were as colorful as its name. One of its regiments was the old New York National Guard 69th Infantry, renumbered the 165th Regiment. The "Fighting 69th" had a glorious tradition. Made up mostly of Irish-Americans from New York City, it had been in the thick of the fighting during the Civil War. Its colonel was William "Wild Bill" Donovan, who'd go on to lead the OSS (Office of Strategic Services), America's spy and sabotage service during the Second World War. Under Donovan, the Fighting 69th became one of the AEF's most decorated outfits.

The Rainbow's assistant commander was thirty-seven-year-old Colonel Douglas MacArthur, future chief of American forces in the South Pacific in the Second World War. The Doughboys of 1918 loved "Doug" MacArthur. He called them his "buddies"; they called him "The Fighting Dude" and "The Bravest of the Brave." He deserved both names.

MacArthur was a dude, a man who always fussed about his clothes. Since the regulation uniform wasn't flashy enough for him, he made certain "improvements." He removed the wire stiffener from his cap and wore it smashed-down. The rest of his getup was a four-foot-long woolen scarf knitted by his mother, a turtleneck sweater with the West Point insignia, skintight riding breeches, and cavalry boots polished mirror-bright.

Yet the Dude was fearless, and everyone from Black Jack down knew it. General Charles Menoher, the Rainbow's commander, said: "MacArthur is the bloodiest fighting man in the army. There's no risk of battle that any soldier is called upon to take that he is not liable to look up and see Mac-Arthur at his side." When patrols went on midnight raids across no-man's-land, MacArthur led them, armed only with a riding crop. He refused to carry a gas mask, considering it ugly and undignified; nor would he rumple his neatly combed hair with a helmet.

At St.-Mihiel MacArthur was the first officer to leap out of the trenches and lead his men forward. Later that morning he and Major Patton were watching the advance when shells began dropping around them. Each man, priding himself on his courage, wouldn't give the other the satisfaction of seeing him take cover. They just stood there, looking each other in the eye and talking about nothing in particular, as the explosions grew louder. Then MacArthur saw Patton flinch for an instant and look annoyed with himself. "Don't worry, Major," he said, grinning, "you never hear the one that gets you."

The Dude believed he led a charmed life and that nothing could kill him. That day his men occupied a mansion that had been a German general's headquarters. The general had resented losing such nice quarters and decided that the Americans shouldn't enjoy them either. MacArthur had just sat down to lunch with his staff when shells started landing in the courtyard. His staff dove for cover, as any sensible person would. Not their chief. He stood ramrod-straight, muttering, "All of Germany cannot make a shell than can kill Mac-Arthur. Sit down, gentlemen, with me." His luck was contagious, and they finished the meal without the shells coming closer. Whether they enjoyed it is another matter.

MacArthur's heroism made him the most decorated battle-field commander in the AEF. In addition to winning the

Silver Star seven times, he held the Distinguished Service Cross, Purple Heart, and Croix de Guerre.

Things went so well that the Battle of St.-Mihiel was nearly over by sundown. As the French liberated St.-Mihiel itself, American units advancing from the north and south sides of the salient met in the middle. The following two days were spent in mopping up pockets of resistance and gathering loot.

There was plenty to gather. In addition to 23,000 prisoners, the Germans lost 450 cannon and thousands of tons of valuable supplies. Of the 7,000 Yank casualties, most were lightly wounded. The ambulance trains chugged away from St.-Mihiel nearly empty.

When Pershing received news of the victory, an aide recalled him being "happy as a clam." But only briefly, for he remembered his promise to Marshal Foch.

"Everyone attack as soon as they can, as strong as they can, for as long as they can. *Tout le monde à la bataille!*—Everyone into the battle!"

Foch coined this slogan to describe his plan for the knockout blow against Germany. The big offensive was scheduled to begin September 26 with a massive American drive toward Sedan and the southern section of the Antwerp-Metz railway. On each succeeding day, the French, British, and Belgians would go over the top. They were to hammer away, ignoring losses, until they broke through the Hindenburg Line.

In order to be ready on time, the entire American First Army had to sideslip from St. Mihiel behind French-held Verdun. Later, battle-scarred veterans shuddered when they recalled the move to the new sector. They marched only at night, after heavy rains had turned the dirt roads into streams of mud. Military policemen shouted themselves hoarse directing traffic over the din of sloshing boots and chugging motors. Smoking was forbidden, since glowing cigarettes were visible to scout planes. Vehicle lights were painted over, except for a tiny square in the center covered with blue paper; without these specks of light, drivers couldn't have kept in line.

The center of each road was a jumble of trucks, rolling kitchens, water wagons, ambulances, tanks, cannon, and ammunition caissons. From time to time there was a loud crash as a piece of heavy equipment skidded into a ditch. The column bunched up, remaining nearly motionless until the obstacle was removed. If it couldn't be righted quickly, it was heaved off the road and left for junk. Sweating mule skinners encouraged their animals with shouts and curses. Animals that slipped and broke a leg, or collapsed from fatigue, were shot.

The infantry trudged along the roadsides, where the mud was deepest. Some, their rifles slung over their shoulders, had loaves of bread skewered on the bayonets; they were too bulky to fit into backpacks and too precious to be left behind. Now and then a Doughboy took a swig of brandy from his canteen; it should have been filled with water, but brandy was cheap and it warmed your insides in the cold dampness. Army old-timers squirted streams of yellow chewing-tobacco juice from between clenched teeth.

As the first rays of sunlight purpled the horizon, the marching columns left the roads. During the day they slept in the dripping woods and ate cold monkey meat, as cooking fires might alert the enemy to the build-up. By nightfall, when the march resumed, tempers were frayed. Grumbling led to insults, which led to fights, until the sergeants stepped in.

Traffic jam. Military transport of all kinds clogs a road in preparation of the Meuse–Argonne offensive. Sometimes the columns moved forward at two miles an hour.

Superhuman effort, aided by Colonel Marshall's planning, brought the First Army to its destination on time. By the evening of September 25, 1918, it stood ready to launch the Battle of the Meuse-Argonne.

The battle takes its name from the American sector, a twenty-one-mile front running eastward from the Meuse River above Verdun to the western edge of the Argonne Forest. The country here is perfect for defense, the best anywhere on the Western Front. The ground falls off sharply from the heights of the Meuse to a valley broken by rugged hills, rising again to the plateau of the Argonne. The steep, wooded hillsides along the Meuse and Argonne plateau were held by the enemy, who could catch the Americans in a crossfire as they moved up the valley. The Argonne Forest itself was a boulder-strewn wilderness of giant trees and thick underbrush, like Belleau Wood, only twenty times larger. It would be a tough nut to crack.

Nine American divisions were strung out from right (east) to left (west) across the front: the 33rd, 80th, 4th, 79th, 37th, 91st, 35th, 28th, 77th. Waiting in reserve were the Big Red One, Rainbow, and 32nd, or Flaming Arrow, divisions. Behind them were thousands of airmen, gunners, supply troops, and medical personnel. Altogether over a million-and-a-quarter Yanks awaited Black Jack's signal to move forward.

The big push began with a sound like the crack of doom. A few seconds after midnight, September 25, four thousand guns opened fire. Before they finished this preliminary bombardment, the Americans would drop forty thousand tons of shells on the German positions, more than all the cannon ammunition fired by the Union Army during the Civil War.

The guns pounded the Germans until five o'clock the next morning, when the artillerymen lowered their sights to con-

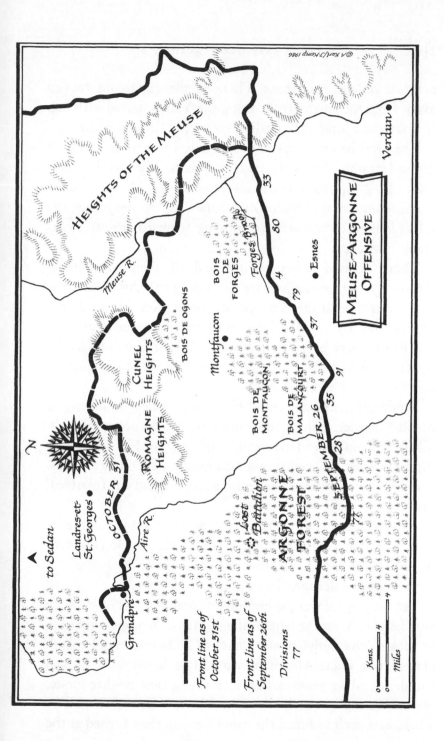

© A. Karl / J. Kemp 1986

MEUSE–ARGONNE OFFENSIVE

HEIGHTS OF THE MEUSE

Meuse R.

Forges Brook

BOIS DE FORGES

Montfaucon

BOIS DE OGONS

CUNEL HEIGHTS

ROMAGNE HEIGHTS

BOIS DE MONTFAUCON

BOIS DE MALANCOURT

ARGONNE FOREST

Lost Battalion

Aire R.

OCTOBER 31

Landres-et-St. Georges

Grandpré

to Sedan

N

Verdun

Esnes

33

80

4

79

37

91

35

28

77

SEPTEMBER 26

Front line as of October 31st

Front line as of September 26th

Divisions   77

Kms.   0   4
Miles   0   4

centrate on the rear areas. Then, as the explosions moved away from the enemy front lines, the Yanks started walking. It was to be a long walk, ending six weeks later in victory.

The Germans were taken completely by surprise and gave ground steadily during the next two days. The assault troops were in high spirits and sang about how "We'll hang out the washing on the old Hindenburg Line." In the meantime, the Allies launched their attacks, moving forward against weakening resistance.

Then German resistance stiffened all along the Meuse-Argonne front, becoming hard as stone. Jerry, his back to the wall, fought with the courage of desperation. He made the Doughboys pay in blood for every yard of ground gained.

The offensive began to bog down. If it stalled completely, the entire Allied effort would be endangered, prolonging the war for at least another year.

Pershing became desperate. He drove his field commanders to push harder, harder. But most of all he drove himself. There was no relief from work and worry. He sped along slippery roads at seventy miles an hour to encourage, to advise, to bully. Wherever he went, a second staff car followed, just in case the first broke down.

At times the strain became almost unbearable. One evening, while driving through a cold drizzle, Black Jack suddenly put his hands over his face. "My God," he sobbed, "I sometimes wonder how I can go on."

Yet busy as he was, he couldn't forget the loss of his wife and daughters. At the height of the Meuse-Argonne fighting, he took a drive with Colonel Charles G. Dawes, an old friend. Dawes, too, knew what it meant to lose loved ones; his son had drowned six years earlier. For a long time neither spoke, but sat staring out of his own window, wrapped in gloom. Then, as if each had read the other's mind, they turned at the

Advance through the Argonne. A two-man team fires a cannon during a battle; the gun, though tiny compared to Long Toms, fired a one-pound shell that could do a lot of damage to troops caught in the open. The part of the forest they are fighting in looks as if it had been swept by a great blaze.

same moment. Each was crying. "Even this war can't keep it out of my mind," said Black Jack.

A general's battle plan is the overall picture; it outlines who will do what, when, and why. But the actual battle is never so orderly; it is made up of countless pieces, separate actions that fit together to give shape to the whole. Sometimes one of these actions becomes a cherished part of a nation's heritage. And so it was with the six-day ordeal of the "Lost Battalion" of the Argonne Forest.

One of the units Pershing ordered to push harder was the 77th Infantry Division. Known as the Melting Pot Division, the 77th was a New York City outfit with a Statue of Liberty emblem on its shoulder patch. Its men spoke forty-three languages, including Chinese, Yiddish, Arabic, German, Italian, and Gaelic.

The men of the Melting Pot took pride in themselves and their city. One night, as their columns passed those of the Rainbow marching in opposite directions, soldiers yelled out their sections of the city and cheered the answering cries. Bronx. Brooklyn. Little Italy. Someone started to bellow "The Sidewalks of New York," and soon the night echoed with "East Side, West Side, all around the town. . . ."

The New Yorkers had seen plenty of action, but nothing like the job Black Jack handed them this time. They were to bulldoze their way through the Argonne as quickly as possible. Their units were to keep moving even though they lost touch with those to the right and left. If the enemy attacked their flanks, that was too bad; they must knock him down and keep moving.

One of the units to attack along the western edge of the Argonne was a six-hundred-man battalion drawn from various regiments. Its commander was Major Charles Whittlesey, a New Englander who practiced law in Wall Street. A tall thin man with thick glasses, he looked like a young Woodrow Wilson. Stern and unsmiling, he was a stickler for discipline. "Galloping Charlie" wasn't (yet) one of the AEF's most beloved officers.

First day. Wednesday, October 2, 1918. Whittlesey followed his orders to the letter. With a pistol in one hand and wirecutters in the other, he led his men into the forest.

The battalion advanced easily—*too* easily. After over-

Major Charles ("Galloping Charlie") Whittlesey was a New York lawyer who led the Lost Battalion during the Meuse–Argonne offensive.

running a lightly held German position, it met no resistance. Whittlesey wondered why things were going so easily, but was thankful that losses were light.

Toward nightfall, the battalion climbed a hill, went down the slope to Charlevaux Brook, and crossed a wooden footbridge. They found themselves at the bottom of a steep ravine covered with thick woods on either slope. Just before dark, Whittlesey had everyone dig in for the night on the ravine's northern slope, below a road dating from Roman times.

Whittlesey's eyelids were growing heavy when he heard boots snapping twigs nearby. "Beg pardon, sir," said a sergeant, "but Private Powers thinks he heard someone speaking German back where we just came from."

The major squeezed his eyes shut for a moment, then opened them. "Private Powers is having nightmares," he snapped. "Tell him to go back to sleep." But Whittlesey couldn't follow his own order. He lay awake, wondering, worrying. Star shells flickering in the distance told him that the enemy was still in the Argonne. But where? And how near?

Whittlesey was right to be concerned. Although he couldn't know it then, his battalion was being surrounded. He'd not only advanced beyond the 77th, but had stumbled through a small gap in the enemy line. As he lay awake in his foxhole, an entire German regiment closed the gap. The Lost Battalion was never lost. Its commander knew its exact location; and, at dawn, so did the enemy.

Second day. Thursday, October 3, 1918. The Doughboys awoke to the chirping of birds and the crash of *Minenwerfer*, mortar shells. Machine guns began crackling from every direction.

The Doughboys were in the worst possible position. Enemy troops held the high ground, firing downward from behind trees and boulders. It was like shooting fish in a barrel.

Whittlesey issued two orders. The men were to dig their foxholes deeper. Their officers were also to make them understand, "Our mission is to hold this position at all costs."

Soon they learned what "at all costs" meant. Whittlesey sent out several patrols to probe for an opening in the German line. It was always the same: a few minutes passed, then machine-gun bursts, explosions, and silence.

The enemy showed himself in the afternoon. The Yanks, huddled in their foxholes, could hear movement in the underbrush. Suddenly there was a shout, *"Nun, alle zusammen!"*— "Now, all together!" Gray-clad figures bounded from the woods, hurling grenades as they came.

The explosions crept nearer, but the Yanks lay low, wait-

Doughboys dug in along a hillside in the Argonne Forest. Notice the hole in the helmet in the foreground; its wearer was probably shot in the head.

ing. No one gave the order to fire, but as the Germans came in range, they ran into a hail of bullets. Some shrieked, crumpling to the ground. Grenades went off at the feet of enemy soldiers shot before they could throw them. The enemy had enough. He faded into the forest and treated the Yanks to a diet of *Minenwerfer* shells and sniper bullets until sunset.

Nobody sang "The Sidewalks of New York" that night. It was a night of pain and misery. German snipers, invisible in the darkness, lay prone on the hillsides. Every groan from the wounded, every tinkling of metal, brought a couple of bullets. Captain George McMurtry, who'd been shot in the knee, crawled among the wounded. Fighting back the pain, he whispered to each man, "Everything is practically okay." He begged a youngster, shot in the stomach, to keep still. "It pains like hell, Captain," he said, "but I'll keep as quiet as a can." He died a half-hour later without making another sound.

The battalion had fought bravely, but everyone knew what they were up against. Besides being outnumbered by better than five to one, their supplies were dangerously low. Food was nearly gone, as were medical supplies. Already the medics were going through the pockets of the dead for first-aid packets.

Whittlesey wrote a message to report his position and ask for an airdrop of supplies; most of all, he needed artillery support to break the encirclement. The message was then attached to the leg of a carrier pigeon, who landed in its coop near the 77th's headquarters. American outfits in the Argonne had no field telephones, relying on runners or carrier pigeons for their communications.

Third day. Friday, October 4, 1918. This was to be the worst day of the siege. It would torture the survivors' dreams for the rest of their lives.

The day began as usual, with a hail of *Minenwerfer* shells crashing among the foxholes and snipers shooting at anything that moved. Late in the afternoon, however, a plane appeared overhead. It looped and dived, its red, white, and blue insignia clearly visible. The pilot fired a signal rocket and flew away. Whittlesey's men laughed and clapped each other on the back. Help was coming.

No, it wasn't. Instead of a supply-drop, they heard loud screeching. Shells! And the noise came from the south, the American lines. The Long Toms were limbering up for action.

War is full of accidents. When millions of men struggle with powerful weapons, something always goes wrong. A defective grenade may explode in its owner's hand when he pulls the pin. Pilots strafe their own ground troops. Artillerymen misjudge their aim and drop shells on their own troops. This is called "friendly fire," although the shells kill just the same as if they came from enemy guns.

Someone, somehow, had made a terrible error. The Lost Battalion began to receive a heavy dose of friendly fire. Shells hit trees, sending them toppling over as if felled by a giant axe. Shells landed in foxholes. One man vanished in a flash; another had his chest blown out by an American shell.

Everyone tried frantically to dig himself deeper into the ground—everyone, that is, except Galloping Charlie. He was on his feet, bounding from foxhole to foxhole. "Take it easy, there, take it easy," he said to a whimpering Doughboy. "We're all right. This won't last long."

Rushing toward the headquarters hole, he motioned the pigeon man to follow him with his birdcage. Whittlesey's message said it all: "We're along the road parallel 276.4. Our artillery is dropping a barrage directly on us. For heaven's sake, stop it." The message was clipped to the leg of Cher Ami, the last pigeon, the Lost Battalion's last link with the outside world. Cher Ami is French for "Dear Friend." And that little bird proved itself the dearest of friends that day.

Not that it seemed that way at first. Cher Ami rose into the air and then, for some bird's-own reason, settled on the limb of a blasted tree. The major and its keeper threw pebbles at it, ducking all the while from the shellbursts. At last Cher Ami took off and flew away. The Germans, seeing it leave the American position, turned all their guns on the tiny creature.

Cher Ami saved the day. It arrived at its loft with an eye gone, its breastbone shattered, and a leg shot away. But it arrived with Whittlesey's message. The barrage was called off after four hours.

Eighty Yanks lay dead or wounded due to friendly fire. Yet the survivors would never look at their commander in the same way as before. There was a lot more to Galloping Charlie than they thought. Sure, he was strict, but also fair; he never asked anyone to do what he wouldn't do himself. He took risks above and beyond the call of duty to help others. He walked around the position, ignoring pinging bullets, to give them encouragement. He always found time to comfort the wounded or give them a sip of water. That night the Lost Battalion realized that it loved its major.

Fourth day. Saturday, October 5, 1918. At 10 o'clock Whittlesey's men heard the whooshing of the "incoming mail" of Long Toms from the south. Every head turned toward the sound, wondering if they were going to be blasted with friendly fire again.

A line of explosions, perfectly straight, erupted in front of their position.

There was another line of them, closer. "Oh, my God, again?" men muttered, breaking into a sweat despite the morning chill.

Then a torrent of shells poured into the hillside beyond, right into the enemy. The explosions danced along the treetops, above the Germans' heads. Amid the zinging fragments of steel, the Doughboys heard screams of terror and pain. Chunks of bodies and scraps of uniform flew above the treetops. They cheered for, as one said, there's nothing as good as seeing a person who's bullied you getting the same from a bigger bully. But the cheering stopped along with the bombardment, and the *Minenwerfer* took over until sundown.

Fifth day. Sunday, October 6, 1918. Time was running out for the Lost Battalion. The last scraps of food had been eaten two days earlier and the men were starving. Those who could manage it gnawed the bark off trees or munched handfuls of grass; a lucky few nibbled on wax candles. Men were so weak from hunger and groggy from lack of sleep that it was hard to walk even a couple of steps. Men would rise, only to trip on a pebble. The medics ran out of painkiller and bandages. Fresh wounds had to be covered with dressings taken from the dead and folded so the old bloodstain didn't touch the new wound.

At midday thirteen American planes dropped food packages to the Lost Battalion. Corned Willie, monkey meat, butter, biscuits, chocolate, cigarettes rained from heaven. The famished men watched the food parcels come down—right into the German positions. The Germans, who hadn't seen such delicacies in months, were grateful for the early Christmas presents. When an inexperienced machine gunner aimed at the planes, a veteran knocked him down, shouting "Don't shoot the delicatessen-flyers!"

The Germans, refreshed by the fine food, ended the day with a flamethrower attack. Storm Troopers charged from the woods behind streamers of orange fire. That was a mistake, for the Yanks, angry at losing their food drop, took out their anger on the flamethrower teams. None survived.

Sixth day. Monday, October 7, 1918. Everyone knew that today would probably be the Lost Battalion's last. The men's strength was nearly gone, except for what it took to pull a trigger. Their position smelled, a combination of unwashed bodies and decay; the men were too weak to bury the dead, simply covering them with leaves and twigs.

Whittlesey decided to send a message through one last

The big push. A machine gun company of the Big Red One moves up to the front. The paths behind them are thick with advancing Doughboys.

time. Since there weren't any more carrier pigeons, men would have to do the job. Any volunteers?

Three men slipped out of their foxholes early in the morning. Unarmed, slithering on their bellies, they disappeared into the underbrush. An hour later, shots rang out in the distance. Two men crawled back into the American position soon afterward. The woods bristled with machine guns, they reported. Impossible to get through. They'd lost touch with the third man, Abe Krotoshinsky, a small, stoop-shouldered fellow from the slums of the Lower East Side. Probably dead.

There was nothing left to do but prepare for a last stand. Exhausted men with bloodshot eyes began sharpening bayonets on pieces of stone. Men in stiffened bandages brushed the dirt from their last cartridges. Before they "went West"

—died—they meant to send a flock of Germans ahead of them.

In the meantime, Black Jack had ordered an all-out effort to rescue the Lost Battalion. The Big Red One came out of reserve, and together with the Bloody Buckets* of the 28th Infantry Division slammed into the Argonne from the east; that is, to the left and rear of the besieging Germans. The enemy commander, fearing that he'd be encircled himself, released his grip on the Lost Battalion.

Late that afternoon a man wriggled into one of the 77th's forward machine gun posts. He was small and stoop-shouldered, and he babbled disjointed phrases: "gimme . . . eats . . . grub . . . drink." As he was wolfing down a can of Corned Willie, someone recognized him. Abe Krotoshinsky, K Company. He hadn't been killed by the machine guns, only stunned momentarily.

It was night when Abe led a relief company to his buddies. They smelled them before they saw them. The first man into the position slipped into a foxhole in the dark, inches away from a bayonet that flashed by his throat. When the man with the bayonet realized who the stranger was, he went down on his knees. Another man lay in the foxhole, covered with bloody bandages. "See?" he said, cradling him in his arms. "We're relieved. You're going to be all right."

Of the 600 who'd marched with Galloping Charlie, 107 died and 194 were able to walk out with their rescuers; the rest went to the hospital. Whittlesey was promoted to lieutenant colonel and awarded the Medal of Honor.

Cher Ami also had its reward. The hero-pigeon went on to become a celebrity. The French gave it the Croix de Guerre. Black Jack ordered that it be returned to the United

---

* The 28th's insignia was a red keystone resembling a blood-filled bucket.

States in a private cabin aboard the transport *Ohioan*. It received the best medical treatment the country could offer, including a beautifully carved wooden leg. When Cher Ami died in 1919, its body was stuffed and put on honorable display in the Smithsonian Institution in Washington, D.C.

The day following the Lost Battalion's rescue, a Doughboy fought a one-man battle in another part of the Argonne Forest. Black Jack would call him "the greatest civilian soldier of the war" and recommend him for the Medal of Honor.

Alvin Cullum York never expected to win medals. A tall, redheaded mountaineer of twenty-seven, he hailed from Pall Mall, Tennessee. After spending his youth gambling and brawling, he became interested in religion and joined the local church. Overnight he changed from a roughneck into a quiet, gentle man. His neighbors never knew him to drink alcohol, smoke tobacco, or use bad language. Although his fists were hard as bowling balls, and he could shoot out a squirrel's eye at fifty yards, he'd never harm another person. He was a man of peace, believing with all his heart that God wants us to love one another.

One day the postman brought Alvin's draft notice. It was as if a ton of bricks had fallen on him. "I can't tell you how it felt," he wrote later in his autobiography. "I just can't describe it. I was all mussed up. Everything was going from under me. Fight! Kill! And I'd been converted to the Gospel of peace and love, and of 'Do good for evil.' "

He walked the mountains night after night, alone, trying to puzzle things out. He read his Bible and prayed for guidance. Yet no answers came. He could have fled deeper into the mountains, where no government man could have found him. But Alvin York had never run away from anything,

and surely not from his own country. Killing was evil; that
he knew. The law must be obeyed; that he also knew. So he
reported to camp as the draft notice ordered.

York was the best trainee in his company. He followed
orders, putting others to shame on the target range. But he
made the officers understand that targets weren't people.
He'd never shoot another person whatever they ordered.

One night his company commander took him to see the
major to talk things over. After hours of debating back and
forth, Major Buxton convinced him that he could be a good
person and a good soldier at the same time. The Allies were
fighting a just war and, as an American, it was his duty to
serve in that struggle. York agreed, promising to do his best.
By the time his outfit arrived in France, he'd earned corporal's stripes.

Corporal York belonged to Company C, 328th Infantry
Regiment, 82nd Infantry Division. His division was nicknamed the "All-American." Although made up mostly of
southerners—Georgians, Alabamians, Tennesseans—it included men from many other states as well. An experienced
division, it had been hardened by weeks of combat against
some of the best outfits in the kaiser's army.

On October 8, 1918, York was part of a twenty-one-man
squad patrolling behind an enemy machine gun battalion.
Moving Indian-style, from tree to tree, they saw a group of
twenty Germans relaxing in a clearing. Before the Germans
could catch their breath, Doughboys were motioning for
them to reach for the sky—or else. Their leader, a major, felt
the cold barrel of a Colt .45 at the back of his head.

Suddenly machine gunners on a low hill opposite to the
clearing began to fire. The first bursts killed six Yanks and
wounded six others, including the sergeant in charge; one
man fell riddled with a hundred bullets that tore off his

Sergeant Alvin C. York on the hillside where he matched his rifle against German machine guns.

clothes. Corporal York, the quiet man who loved peace, was now in command and responsible for his men's lives.

As the others hugged the ground, he crawled forward, taking cover behind a mossy log. One man faced at least ten machine guns with a combined firepower of five thousand bullets a minute. York's rifle fired a six-shot clip. The machine gunners never had a chance.

This Tennessean had grown up in the forest with a rifle. He knew how to hide and stalk and shoot from cover. In order to aim, the Germans had to raise their heads above the sandbags that protected their machine gun nests. Each time a man peered out, the forest hunter squeezed off a single shot. It always found its mark. "I jest teched 'em off," York recalled. Soon a dozen Germans lay slumped over their weapons.

York had fired his twelfth shot when six Germans, led by an officer, charged him with fixed bayonets. He had only three shots left in his rifle, and they were coming awfully fast.

Again he used a hunter's trick. Instead of shooting the man in front, which would have made the others take cover, he picked off the last man, then the next-to-last and so on, so that the leaders didn't know their companions were down. When his rifle was empty, he whipped out his .45 and downed the others.

York, keep in mind, wasn't attacking anyone, only defending his own people strenuously. Reloading his rifle, he kept after the machine gunners. He'd shoot a few, then yell for their comrades to surrender; he didn't want to kill any more than necessary. Perhaps they didn't understand his Tennessee drawl, for they kept firing and he kept "teching" them off.

During a lull in the fighting, the captured German major heard his demand for surrender. He promised that if York spared his men, he'd order them to surrender. York agreed, and the major blew a whistle. About thirty men stood up, hands above their heads, and came down the bloodsoaked hillside. One foolishly hid a small grenade in his fist, which he threw at York's head. But it missed, wounding a prisoner. York shot him too, although he admired his courage.

By now he had fifty prisoners. He ordered some to pick up the American wounded, placing the rest in front of them as a screen. "I wasn't a-goin' to leave any good American boys lying out there to die. . . . And I taked the major and placed him at the head of the column and I got behind him and used him as a screen. I poked the Colt in his back and told him to hike. And he hiked."

Whenever they came to a cluster of machine gun nests, the corporal made the major blow his whistle. Each batch was promptly disarmed and put in line with the others. After an hour of whistle-blowing, the column was a mass of gray flecked with brown. York's only worry was that the American artillery might mistake them for an enemy counterattack and open fire. He felt a lot better when they reached the 82nd's outposts without a shot being fired.

"Well, York," said Brigadier General Lindsay, grinning from ear to ear. "I hear you have captured the whole damned German army."

"Nossir," the Tennessean replied, "I only have one hundred thirty-two."

Only one hundred thirty-two! With that the general's grin became a roar of laughter. York had also brought back thirty-five German machine guns. Left behind were thirty dead enemy soldiers, more or less.

They gave Alvin York the Medal of Honor and the third stripe of a sergeant. He returned home a hero and could have made a fortune retelling his story on the stage. Nothing doing! He hadn't gone to war for publicity or to win medals. He took up farming outside Pall Mall, married the girl he'd courted before the war, and raised money for a school so that the mountain folk would be better educated than he had been. He never understood why people raised such a fuss about what he'd done. "I wanted to do the best I could" was his only comment.

The Meuse-Argonne offensive continued throughout October. The Yank divisions advanced slowly, a series of battering rams smashing northward along parallel lines. Enemy strongpoints in the valley—Montfoucon, Cunel Heights, Romagne Heights—were overrun after desperate fighting. The Argonne was completely cleared with the capture of Grandpré at its northern end.

Colonel Marshall set the pace of the advance from his office at First Army headquarters. Marshall found ways to keep up the pressure, never giving the Germans time to rest and reorganize. Fresh outfits from the reserve were passed through the lines to give tired divisions a few days' relaxation. In this way the Big Red One, Rainbow, and Flaming Arrow took their turn with the enemy.

The Rainbow joined the battle in time to face the most difficult obstacle of all. Beyond the valley, barring the Yanks' path, lay a series of ridges, one behind the other, rising to higher and higher ground. The Kriemhilde Fortress commanded the crest of the highest ridge. Named after a witch in a German legend, this fortress was the southernmost position of the Hindenburg Line. The place bristled with gun emplacements. As one Doughboy said of the Kriemhilde, "Every blankety-blank German there who didn't have a machine gun had a cannon."

Wild Bill Donovan's Fighting 69th spearheaded the Rainbow's assault. The going was rougher than anything these veterans had experienced thus far. They'd attack a strongpoint in the morning, capture it in the afternoon, and lose it to a counterattack by evening. Father Francis Duffy, the regiment's chaplain, had his hands full, comforting the wounded and saying prayers for the dead.

Donovan drove his regiment as Black Jack drove the whole First Army. He was always in front, leading the way without thinking of the danger or his personal safety. He'd stand in the open, reading his map, ignoring the bullets kicking up dust around his feet. Although he expected to be killed in battle, it never bothered him or caused him to lose a moment's sleep. A deeply religious man, he'd made his peace with God and was prepared for anything. That feeling of confidence earned him the Medal of Honor.

On the night of October 14–15, the Fighting 69th was dug in to repel an enemy counterattack. Wild Bill was making the rounds of the various units when—*whack!* It felt as if a demon hit him in the leg with a spiked club. The bullet's

Colonel William ("Wild Bill") Donovan of the Fighting 69th. During the Meuse–Argonne offensive, Donovan stuck to his post in spite of a painful knee wound.

force knocked him down, and after a few minutes he managed to crawl to his command post.

Nobody would have said a word had he asked to be evacuated. His knee was smashed and waves of pain ran from it through his whole body. But Donovan stayed at the front; indeed, he wouldn't let the first-aid men tell anyone he was wounded. The Germans were expected any moment, and he had to be with his men. If he left, or if they learned of his wound, they might lose heart and retreat. Wild Bill remained in his dugout for five hours, as the pain increased, waiting for the enemy.

At last they came. Storm Troopers bolted from the blackness, shooting and bayoneting everyone in their path. The fight seesawed back and forth, neither side willing to give up until the wounded colonel turned the tide. Donovan grabbed his bullhorn, shouting, "They can't get me, and they can't get you." That battle cry, rising above the noise of battle, brought the Fighting 69th to its feet in a wild bayonet charge. Only when the enemy was driven back did he allow the stretcher bearers to take him away.

Donovan was recovering in the hospital when Douglas MacArthur was given command of the Rainbow. At thirty-eight, the Dude was the youngest American divisional head. In a series of fierce head-on assaults, he stormed the Kriemhilde Fortress and the half-completed position to the east.

They were through. Not only the Americans, but the other Allies were winning their objectives. The French, advancing on the Doughboys' left, liberated more and more of their country from the invader. To the north, at Cambrai, the British broke the Hindenburg Line with tanks and infantry. The Belgians swept over Ypres Ridge and took Ghent, the great city southwest of Antwerp.

They were through. Behind them lay the trenches and the

wastes of no-man's-land. Ahead of them lay open country and the fleeing Germans. The war of stalemate suddenly became one of swift, deadly movement.

Each morning the guns roared. Doughboys, Tommies, and poilus burst from cover, driving the enemy eastward, always eastward. There were no more battles, only day-long chases. The galloping artillery horses and bouncing caissons could barely keep up with the pursuit.

By November 7, the Rainbow stood on the heights of the Meuse, across from Sedan. MacArthur's gunners began dropping shells on the Antwerp-Metz railway, making it unusable for the Germans. Next day the Rainbow stood aside to give the French the honor of retaking their long-lost city.

The Meuse-Argonne campaign was over. The Yanks had paid a fearful price, 132,000 killed and wounded, but they'd delivered the knockout blow.

German morale cracked, along with the defenses of the Hindenburg Line. Enough was enough. Brave men tossed away their weapons and ran for their lives. Others, too tired to run, threw up their hands, crying *"Kamerad!"* Each day thousands surrendered and were herded into prisoner-of-war compounds in the rear. Many were youngsters, barely out of high school, or men in their early fifties, a sure sign that the enemy was nearing collapse.

The first week of November 1918 was the worst the German nation had experienced in centuries. Disaster followed disaster. Ludendorff resigned, changed into civilian clothes, and slipped over the border to neutral Sweden. Mutiny broke out in the fleet at Kiel, followed by revolution in Germany's major cities. By week's end, civilians were battling police in Berlin; soldiers on leave often joined the rioters. People, hungry and war-weary, turned on their government.

The government had no choice but to ask for an armistice, or ceasefire, based on President Wilson's peace program. Known as The Fourteen Points, this program called for an end to secret treaties, for freedom of the seas, and the return of enemy-occupied territory. The most important point was the last, a demand for a League of Nations. Wilson wanted a world organization to abolish war by forcing nations to compromise their differences and to punish peace-breakers.

In the meantime, Kaiser Wilhelm II gave up his throne and fled to neutral Holland. Germany, now a republic, sent a delegation to receive Marshal Foch's armistice terms. They were harsh terms: immediate withdrawal from France and Belgium, surrender of thousands of heavy weapons, Allied occupation of key German cities. The delegation accepted these terms and the Armistice was scheduled to go into effect on the eleventh hour of the eleventh day of the eleventh month: 11:00 A.M., November 11, 1918.

News of the coming armistice swept the Western Front. Excitement began to build the night before it was to go into effect. Yanks cheered and hung the kaiser in effigy. Signs reading "Bad Bill—Gone to Hell" appeared as if by magic.

The battle-torn armies had reason to cheer and sing and make a racket. They'd lived through the First World War, the greatest conflict in the history of humanity.

At American aerodromes men rolled out tanks of gasoline and set them afire, dancing around the leaping flames. Flares of every color shot up from every direction. Searchlights crisscrossed the sky, turning clouds into pools of shimmering silver. "I've lived through the war!" a pilot shouted, dancing alone in the center of a mudhole. "We won't be shot at any more!" a buddy babbled over and over again, waving his arms.

Yet the killing went on until the very last moment. On

Armistice morning, German gunners blazed away, determined to use up their ammunition. Allied gunners answered, but for a different reason. Everyone wanted to fire the war's last shot. Gun crews tied ropes to the firing mechanisms of cannon; then two hundred men pulled on each line at once. Hundreds died during those last few, furious seconds.

At 11:00 A.M. it stopped. An eerie quiet settled over the Western Front.

An hour earlier, Eddie Rickenbacker took off in his Spad. Orders had come that all pilots were grounded that morning. Now, for the first and only time, Rick disobeyed an order. The end of a world war was too good to miss, and he meant to have a bird's-eye view of the event.

Without announcing his destination, he took off, heading for the front lines. Everywhere he saw men in gray and brown and blue crouching in their positions, poised to shoot the enemy on sight.

One minute to eleven. Thirty seconds. Ten seconds. The eleventh hour of the eleventh day of the eleventh month.

Suddenly men stood up, paused for a moment, and came toward each other. Rickenbacker saw them toss helmets into the air, throw away their guns, and wave. As he turned north, he saw Doughboys and Jerries hugging each other, dancing, and exchanging cigarettes.

He flew up to the French sector around Verdun. He could hardly believe his eyes. After four years of butchery and hatred, Frenchmen and Germans were not only hugging each other but kissing each other on both cheeks. The war was over.

Only later, when the nations counted the cost, did the full measure of the tragedy really sink in. The United States lost 112,432 men, with another 230,074 wounded. We were

It's over! Doughboys celebrating the Armistice.

lucky. Altogether the Europeans had nearly ten million killed and another twenty million wounded.

No single previous event cost so much money as the First World War. The United States spent over thirty-five billion dollars; that is, ten times more than the Civil War. Every two days cost the American people as much as the Revolutionary War. The grand total for all the nations was three hundred billion dollars.

The story of the First World War ends as it began, on a note of sadness. For the victory won so dearly did not bring peace, but only planted the seeds of more war. President Wilson's Fourteen Points were tossed aside by European statesmen in favor of gaining power and territory for their countries. The Treaty of Versailles did not heal the war's wounds, but rubbed salt into them. The League of Nations, which Wilson saw as the world's best hope of peace, was rejected by the United States Senate because it might lead us into future wars.

The night before the Armistice, doctors at a German army hospital outside Berlin had the patients brought into the main hall to break the news of their country's defeat. Among the patients was a twenty-nine-year-old who'd been gassed during the fighting in Belgium. A thin man, he seemed lost in his oversized uniform. The only remarkable thing about his ashen face was the large, drooping mustache.

The pastor broke the news, which went to his heart like a dagger. Startled, angry, humiliated, he groped his way along the crowded corridors and threw himself on his bed. Burying his head in the pillow, he began to cry.

At that moment Corporal Adolf Hitler vowed revenge for Germany's defeat.

Some More Books

There are thousands of good books on the First World War. I have listed a few of the best here, including some old ones, because they are classics. Often large libraries have them in their collections; they are well worth searching out and reading.

Army Times, *The Daring Regiments: Adventures of the AEF in World War I.* New York: Dodd, Mead & Co., 1967.

Asprey, Robert B. *At Belleau Wood.* New York: G. P. Putnam's Sons, 1965.

Bailey, Thomas A. and Paul B. Ryan. *The Lusitania Disaster.* New York: The Free Press, 1975.

Barbeau, Arthur E. and Florette Henri. *The Unknown Soldiers: Black American Troops in World War I.* Philadelphia: Temple University Press, 1974.

Baynes, Ernest H. *Animal Heroes of the Great War.* New York: Macmillan, 1925.

Brown, Anthony Cave. *Wild Bill Donovan: The Last Hero.* New York: Times Books, 1982.

Churchill, Allen. *Over Here! An Informal Re-Creation of the Home Front in World War I.* New York: Dodd, Mead & Co., 1968.

Coffman, Edward M. *The War to End War: The American Experience in World War I.* New York: Oxford University Press, 1968.

Ellis, Edward Robb. *Echoes of Distant Thunder: Life in the United States, 1914–1918.* New York: Coward, McCann & Geoghegan, 1975.

Ellis, John. *Eye-Deep in Hell: Trench Warfare in World War I.* New York: Pantheon Books, 1976.

Fredericks, Pierce G. *The Great Adventure: America in the First World War.* New York: E. P. Dutton & Co., 1960.

Gibbons, Floyd. *And They Thought We Wouldn't Fight.* New York: George H. Doran & Co., 1918.

(Grider, John McGavock). *War Birds: The Diary of an Unknown Aviator.* New York: George H. Doran & Co., 1926.

Gurney, Gene. *Five Down and Glory.* New York: Ballantine Books, 1958.

Harris, Robert, and Jeremy Paxman. *A Higher Form of Killing: The Secret Story of Chemical and Biological Warfare.* New York: Hill and Wang, 1982.

Heinl, Robert D., Jr. *Soldiers of the Sea: The United States Marine Corps, 1775–1962.* Annapolis: U.S. Naval Institute Press, 1962.

Hoehling, A. A. and Mary Hoehling. *The Last Voyage of the Lusitania.* New York: Henry Holt & Co., 1956.

Hudson, James J. *Hostile Skies.* Syracuse: Syracuse University Press, 1968.

Johnson, Thomas M. and Fletcher Pratt. *The Lost Battalion.* Philadelphia: Bobbs-Merrill & Co., 1938.

Longstreet, Stephen. *The Canvas Falcons: The Story of the Men and Planes of World War I.* New York: World Publishing Co., 1970.

McCarthy, Joseph. "The Lost Battalion." *American Heritage,* October 1977.

Manchester, William. *American Caesar: Douglas MacArthur, 1880–1964.* Boston: Little, Brown, 1978.

Mason, Herbert Molloy, Jr. *The Lafayette Escadrille.* New York: Random House, 1964.

Norman, Aaron. *The Great Air War.* New York: Macmillan, 1968.

Rickenbacker, Eddie. *Fighting the Flying Circus.* Garden City: Doubleday, 1965.

Rockwell, Paul Ayres. *American Fighters in the Foreign Legion.* Boston: Houghton Mifflin Co., 1930.

Schuon, Karl, ed. *The Leathernecks.* New York: Franklin Watts, 1963.

Simpson, Colin, *The Lusitania.* Boston: Little, Brown, 1972.

Sims, Admiral William. *The Victory at Sea.* Garden City: Doubleday, 1920.

Stallings, Laurence. *The Doughboys: The Story of the AEF, 1917–1918.* New York: Harper & Row, 1963.

Thomason, John W., Jr. *Fix Bayonets!* New York: Charles Scribner's Sons, 1926. (Thomason was a Marine officer at Belleau Wood and elsewhere; his story, illustrated by his own battlefield drawings, is one of the best to come out of the war.)

Waitt, Alden H. *Gas Warfare.* New York: Duell, Sloan & Co., 1942.

York, Alvin C. *Sergeant York: His Own Life Story and War Diary.* Garden City: Doubleday, 1928.

Index